Your Way To Financial Freedom

# It Is Time To Start A
# Restaurant Business

## The Proven Guide to Start, Run, and Grow a Profitable Venture

## DR. JOHNSON MGANGA

# DEDICATION

I would like to dedicate this book to my late mom (Jane) who has been closer to my life no matter the circumstances. I still cherish your love in every minute of my life. I love you, mama.

your life or business; including your family members, friends, pear mates, and others.

Once you commit to reading this book; it means that you are 100 percent understand and possess full agreement that under no circumstances the author is responsible for misses of the contents or any losses of any kind, nature, or magnitude relating to direct or indirect usability of the content of this book. The author or publisher is not reliable to any misbalance of the information that might be originated from any form of inaccuracies of the information, errors of the contents, or omissions about any information from this book. The reader is highly advised to utilize the information from this book as an informative while preparing to seek professional advice when deemed necessary.

Attention

Additional **Books!**

Hello, my dear readers!

Please, allow me to introduce to you my current and new books.

## Existing Books

## Get a Copy From Amazon

Retire Soon With Rental Income

Source Of Revenue With Fewer Efforts

Make Millions in

House Flipping Business

Trucking Business

A Money Making Machine!

# New Books

*They are coming soon. Below are some of their titles:*

Make 6 Figures In Just Three Months
Tax Business

With God All Things Are Possible.
Goodness And Mercy Are Chasing Me Down!

Inclusive Retirement Planning
Every Minute Counts!

Tax Saving Techniques
Loopholes We Always Take For Granted

## Stay Tunes!

# Restaurant Business

## Short-Term Goals To Accomplish

| Date | Goals | Action Y/N |
|------|-------|------------|
|      |       |            |
|      |       |            |
|      |       |            |
|      |       |            |
|      |       |            |
|      |       |            |

# Restaurant Business

## Long-Term Goals To Accomplish

| Date | Goals | Action Y/N |
|------|-------|------------|
|      |       |            |
|      |       |            |
|      |       |            |
|      |       |            |
|      |       |            |
|      |       |            |

# Table of Contents

# ACKNOWLEDGMENTS

I would like to acknowledge the endless contributions made by my family; namely, Jane, Regis, and my wife Enna. Together, they have been encouraging me in every moment of this journey of producing this book. Without their help, this book would not be complete. Dearly, I love you all.

# Introduction

## Why start a restaurant business?

**The list of facts regarding FOOD WE EAT**

- It is recommended that we eat at least three meals a day.
- Generally, cooking food is time-consuming.
- The time we spend at work, taking care of our families, and having room for personal time; all these activities are making the process of cooking three meals a day be almost impossible.
- Moreover, we constantly get tired of eating our homemade meals over and over. We enjoy a new taste in different environments.
- A variety of dining options persuades people to eat out.
- People eat out to enjoy getting together with friends, relatives, coworkers, and strangers.
- Being saved with someone is another primary reason for people to eat out.
- Data shows that most people do not like doing the dishes, especially men.

**Note:** The list is long, but it is not exhaustive.

There are many reasons most people like dining out. The busier our lives become, the more stress we feel. Constantly, new fast-food places and restaurants are popping up on each corner of our cities. This phenomenon keeps happening because there is space to accommodate new business owners. Most of them are experiencing a positive return on investment (ROI) in their businesses and seeing opportunities to open additional locations.

The time of fearing COVID-19 is over, as the pandemic is considered a normal disease that will be around for a long time. People have come to accept this realization. The presence of effective vaccinations has helped ease the pressure of the pandemic.

As the COVID-19 restrictions are gradually lifting, most people have developed a habit of eating out to escape the pressure of being locked in their houses for almost two years. Generally, the number of people dining out is increasing rapidly. The business consulting industry believes the fast response of people dining out is an opportunity for those with bold ideas to venture into the restaurant business.

We are returning to a normal state of life much sooner than we had anticipated. This is a good time to reflect on your future and review your plans. Although the plan to start a restaurant was not on your to-do list, or the time of launching a business is inconvenient, the research data alone gives you the green light to join the industry now. No matter how small your ideas are or the level of readiness to start this business, this book will open your eyes to the many opportunities the restaurant industry offers. This book is for those who think the challenges of starting a new business are beyond their reach. The information covers essential procedures for preparing your ideas and steps of launching a successful business.

Additionally, the book reveals the procedure of operating a stable venture that maximizes positive ROI. The discussion also includes:

- How to set a comprehensive operational structure.
- Learning procedures for building a practical team of staff.
- How to purchase supplies at a reasonable price.
- Inventory control techniques.
- Ways of operating a sound financial system for your business.
- Skills for setting a comprehensive and functional market structure.
- Procedures for growing a successful restaurant business.

In summary, expect to learn a lot of valuable information, enough to guide you in each step of the business launching process.

# Brainstorming Moment!

## How to maximize the benefits of reading this book?

Techniques to help you get the full benefit of reading this book:

- Use color markers to highlight various areas of interest. For instance:
    - Yellow for main reference points.
    - Green for things to share with friends.
    - Orange for things that must be done and so on.
- At the end of each chapter, you have been provided with two forms:
    - **To-do list form:** Utilize this form to write all take-away things that you want to accomplish later.
    - **Read again form:** Instead of inserting many stickers on each page, utilize this section to list points that need additional review.

🔊))Attention

The main goal is to create a pleasant reading environment needed to maximize the productivity of investing in this book.

## Let's get started...

# Chapter One

*"Knowledge is power, it can turn unimaginable things possible.*

*Use it effectively to your advantage in real-time!"*

*Dr. Johnson Mganga*

## Outlook of the restaurant industry

According to the National Restaurant Association, the food industry has started to grow again after the COVID-19 associated hiccups that have happened in the last two years. The industry expects to see a boost in sales that reach $898 billion for the year 2022 alone. The research data shows that the number of people employed in this industry will reach almost 14.9 million. This figure includes front desk associates to corporate managers and will add 400,000 jobs to the economy. More restaurant owners are beginning to see their businesses recover from the pandemic. Furthermore, the future is even brighter than before as the lives of ordinary Americans start to stabilize.

As we have seen in the introduction, Americans love to eat out, and the trend keeps growing at a substantial rate. This concept in conjunction with the data supplied by the National Restaurant Association, reveals the direction of the industry. It indicates a rising threshold for business owners that keep investing in their ventures. Additionally, the statistics are encouraging to prospective owners like you who want to join this business arena. Even though the idea of starting a restaurant in the last two years seemed impossible, as normality gradually reappears, people are reconsidering opening restaurants.

## Why start a restaurant business?

We have seen the life structure of a regular America, one that is covered with a hard-working schedule 24/7/365. This lifestyle takes away the basic characteristics of preparing balanced meals at home. Some of the disadvantages of the current lifestyle are:

- There is no time to prepare a balanced diet of three meals a day.
- The vague schedules do not allow most people to be in their living places all the time.
- Business or family deals and meetings on some occasions; are difficult to conduct in our homes.
- Most people consider eating out as one of the remedies to reduce depression caused by this fast lifestyle we live.
- Lack of variety of food in our homes.
  As a new business owner, you may feel skeptical about joining

any industry if the data is not strong enough to support your dreams. For the food industry, there are two basic things to pay attention to, the market trends of the industry and the sentiment of the customers. Currently, both are seeing promising news to the current and new operators who want to join in.

As long as you have a market niche strong enough to withstand the forces of competitors, there's always room for making decent revenue. If that is true, you can consider starting your business now. Try to share your thoughts with relatives or friends who trust you and come up with solid opinions to support your claims. You need to be smart enough not to start a business while knowing you did not explore adequate research data to assure the chance of success. You need to conduct comprehensive research necessary to develop functional market opportunities. The market with the ability to bring many customers to cover operating expenses and produce satisfactory positive ROI.

## State of art market opportunity

Generally, the market niche can originate from various backgrounds including:

- **Creativity:** If you possess a high level of ingenuity in the food industry and you think your ideas are marketable, you can consider putting them into practice. Try taking a regular dish and revamping it into a new look that is much tastier than the previous one. Also, make the dish inexpensive, more delicious, and less complicated to prepare than your rivals.

- **Passionate cooking:** Some of you have a deep passion for cooking foods and never stop exploring new ideas whenever time allows. If you fall into this category, you can create a well-designed food package that allows you to become a business owner down the road.

- **Food and wine lover:** Assume you are a wine lover, but you do not know how to cook. However, you would jump at the chance of starting a restaurant in your area. Some people who fall into this category either learn how to cook, hire a chef, or partner with someone who has great knowledge of the food industry. It gives you a chance to open a restaurant even though you are not a good cook. Try to utilize all options available to you to overcome barriers around your ambitions of starting a new business much sooner than later.

- **Cordial host:** This is another niche, a few people possess a high level of talent for entertaining others 24/7. They know how to meet the demands of each participant in the group in a very loving and professional manner. When you take this God given gift and combine it with other industry essential factors, the idea of starting your restaurant will be much closer than you imagined.

- **Family recipe:** There are a lot of recipes from seasoned matriarchs that have become good moneymakers. However, before taking your family recipe to the market, ask yourself the following questions:

  - How delicious is the food cooked from those recipes?
  - How marketable is the food?
  - Is the size of the market big enough to produce a substantial profit for a long time?

Most people have one or more powerful talents that they never bother to explore. Without exploration, they will never know their degree of potential in this industry. You do not have to be a superb chef to start making money from your talents. When you think that way, you may also believe there is a restaurant with a business model that cooks food that pleases all customers in a particular area. There is no such restaurant that exists, especially in America, a place that covers a wide range of cultural diversities. If you try specializing in a few types of foods that only target a hand-picked group of customers, I'm sure you'll find success.

## Food specialization

In economics, specialization is defined as a technique used in the production process to focus only on producing a few types of goods or offering selective services to gain *a greater degree of efficiency*. Based on this definition, for your business to produce satisfactory ROI, pick a few types of food that you will be able to cook at a very high-quality standard. The food must be very delicious and keep customers coming back for more.

The general idea here is to only select a few types of food before starting your restaurant. Dismiss the idea that you should know how to cook a variety of dishes before opening a business. In the business world, that idea is outdated and will not make your company profitable.

Since specialization is a rule of thumb in the business arena, you should follow suit to succeed. The chart below helps clarify this point.

# Specialization in the Food industry

| Company | Specialization | Description |
|---------|----------------|-------------|
| Starbucks | Coffee | Other types of foods are just add-ons. |
| Dunkin donuts | Donuts | Other types of foods are just add-ons. |
| KFC | Chicken | Other types of foods are just add-ons. |
| Chipotles | Rice, beans, and meat | Other types of foods are just add-ons. |

These are just a handful of businesses in this industry that have evidence of the profitability of this strategy. Specialization is more applicable to the fast-food industry as well. Restaurant owners understand the advantage of specializing in a few things. In return, they strive to deliver the best service. The fewer products you decide to offer, the more time you have to perfect your meals. This concept makes sense when you factor in the challenges of dealing with competitors in the market. The goal is to develop a business model that your rivals will not be able to withstand. This is one of the market niches you should adopt when necessary. You need to develop a powerful arsenal of market specialization to be unstoppable in the market against your business rivals.

Remember, I do not say it is a bad idea to save various types of foods in your restaurant. The main takeaway point is for you not to wait for so long while practicing how to prepare deliciously; let's say, thirty meals before you think to open a restaurant. Just pick a combination of a few dynamite dishes and move to the next stage of testing your ideas. Make sure to choose the target market before selecting what type of food to sell to customers.

## Presence of various cultural differences

In the restaurant industry, this concept works well, for those who seize the opportunity. It is a game-changer when you choose the right target market. If you are an immigrant that happens to be living among people from your home country, try to explore the niche in which they savor your delicious meals. The dishes should remind them of the food they used to eat back home. Repeat customers coming back for a taste of nostalgia can be profitable. Alternatively, if you happen to know how to cook tasty dishes from a friend's culture, consider opening a constructive dialog to see how to make the opportunity a success.

I have also seen various restaurants that serve food for multicultural customers. Collectively, the owners managed to come up with productive ideas for single dishes that would attract various customers of countless ethnicities. This is another type of creativity you should explore in your area so that you can start your business soon. Dig deep to create productive opportunities where others could not manage to identify their existence. Use your business mindset to see beyond where ordinary people cannot visualize.

## Advantages of a restaurant business

Without a doubt, the industry has many benefits that sustain business owners in the market. Also, the world has seen a variety of new talented business owners starting different types of restaurants in our neighborhoods. Below are some of the benefits of starting a restaurant:

- **Passion:** Rather than holding on to your food-related passions that may gradually fade away, I strongly suggest exploring starting a business to test your desires. Most people who have done so have experienced positive outcomes. Once you are compelled to enter the business arena, a small vision can be a great source of income. The primary question is, how long are your passions going to last or put it into practice in real-time and start making money?

- **Grandma's recipe:** Most families possess valuable recipes that can be a market niche to start a profitable business. So far, the industry has experienced several successful restaurants that started with family recipes. It is the right time to explore the formulae. You must evaluate the possibilities of multiplying them into a chain of restaurants.

- **Be your own boss:** Unfortunately, most people start a business with many key purposes in mind, including the freedom of becoming a boss. They want to have all the advantages of deciding what type of schedule to follow, who to hire, hours they are going to work, and the kind of food to cook. Are you one of them? If the answer is yes, what are you waiting for? Join the business club right now.

- **Low barrier to entry:** Generally, the industry does not possess harsh restrictions as you find in other industries. The existing rules to follow before opening a restaurant are often common for an ordinary person to navigate.

- **Preserve culture:** The industry has allowed people from various backgrounds to preserve their cultures, especially when it comes to food. Because of this phenomenon, it is common to come across restaurants specializing in cooking foods from one segment of the culture, such as Italian restaurants, Ethiopian cuisine, Chinese food, the taste of Tanzania, and more.

Although the list is not exhaustive, the weight of the benefits is heavy enough to see the need to start your own business. No matter the reasons behind your decision of being a business owner, so long they are within the boundaries of the laws and culture of this country, then follow your gut.

**The cons of starting the restaurant business**

Understandably, the primary aim of pursuing any project is to be able to attain the intended purpose. If making a satisfactory profit is one of the key reasons to start a restaurant, this factor alone is worth discussing the main challenges of this business. I prefer to call them challenges rather than problems or disadvantages. Every determined business-minded person understands that every company has some difficulty executing tasks. It is the primary duty of business owners to find inventive measures to overcome those barriers. When you decide to start a restaurant, expect to face some challenges. A few of these hiccups are:

- **Health and safety:** Both city personnel and customers do not take the safety of food lightly, and you shouldn't either. Constantly strive to stay ahead of all regulations set by the health department to avoid unnecessary fines or business closure.

- **Time commitment:** Operating a restaurant is a time-consuming project that requires full commitment to produce positive results. It depends on your business model. Some owners work full-time to be closer and manage daily business operations.

- **Workforce:** Statistics show how challenging it is to find dedicated employees to work in this industry. The efforts of retaining them also are not easy; due to many factors, including low pay.

- **Managerial experience:** Most managers operating small restaurants; do not possess enough knowledge or experience managing an entity with staff. Lack of managerial skills makes it harder for the management team to control daily business operations, including keeping talented employees.

Generally, it takes time for a brand-new restaurant. That is less known to the community, to start making a profit. The waiting period can be challenging for most owners who have limited savings. Remember, all business expenses must be paid promptly to avoid a shutdown.

Once again, these challenges open the door for prospects to consider all essential factors that play a major role in opening and running a profitable business. These factors will be discussed in the subsequent chapters. Please grasp and utilize them to your advantage. Also, try to avoid rushing to start your dream restaurant without fully completing all major preparations. It is so painful to experience a business burning money soon after being opened due to many factors, including a lack of adequate groundwork. Remember, not all problems are reversible in a timely fashion. So do not be among those taking a risk that is not worth experimenting with.

This chapter has become an eye-opener that is substantial to experience in this fast-growing industry. Research data reveals a lot of potential information that supports the idea of having room for restaurant businesses to keep growing. Also, for the newcomers, the chance of making a sizeable profit is apparent. What is needed is your highest level of commitment and a collective and efficient business model. The time to put your vision into action has arrived. Start by preparing a dedicated business plans and achievable goals before moving the wagon. Furthermore, let the wagon transport you to financial freedom.

# To-Do List Form – Chapter One

| Action | Goals | Results(Y/N) |
|---|---|---|
| Time-sensitive actions:<br><br>1.<br><br>2.<br><br>3.<br><br>4.<br><br>5.<br><br>6.<br><br>7.<br><br>8.<br><br>9.<br><br>10. | | |
| Less time-sensitive actions<br><br>1.<br><br>2.<br><br>3.<br><br>4. | | |

| | | |
|---|---|---|
| 5. | | |
| 6. | | |
| 7. | | |
| 8. | | |
| 9. | | |
| 10. | | |

# Read Again Pages – Chapter One

| Page # | Topic/Subtopic | Purpose | Result (Y/N) |
|--------|----------------|---------|--------------|
|        |                |         |              |
|        |                |         |              |
|        |                |         |              |
|        |                |         |              |
|        |                |         |              |

# Chapter Two

*Do not sit down and wait for opportunities to come.*

*Get up and make them!*

*Madam C. J. Walker*

## Dedicated Restaurant Club

**Here are some crucial questions to ask yourself:**

- Do you have family recipes you want to share for profit?
- Do you love cooking and now want to magnify your dreams?
- Do you have enough passion for preserving your culture, especially at the food level?
- Do you see yourself managing a big chain of restaurants and becoming a boss?

These and other related questions can change the history of your life once you decide to join this business industry. You will find the journey easy and more successful when you form a dedicated restaurant club or become one of the members. Remember, you need the help of the other members to run this business, especially in the beginning stages when there are many challenges to overcome. Sharing the challenges and trying to brainstorm together to come up with practical solutions is one of the essential tenacities of this club.

The point is not for you to start a business partnership with friends but to have close partners willing to share their views candidly. You want to have people who understand the challenges of running a business, especially when you are new in this arena. You can even call it a club of dedicated people willing to support you for a better or worse scenario until your business starts running successfully. You can include your relatives, friends, coworkers, or neighbors. The point is apparent, the more active and dedicated members you have in your club, the easier it will be to start your dream restaurant.

**This is one of the lifetime opportunities you do not want to pass on.**

**Take bold actions right away with the inclusion of your relatives, friends, and coworkers.**

# The sooner the better!

## Why I am sharing the dedicated restaurant club chapter with you?

I love this concept a lot because it is so beneficial more than ever in the business world. Honestly, I did not use it in my first business because I did not have any idea of the advantages of having this type of business club. When I applied it in my house flipping business, it was a game-changer. The greatness of success was enormous and wide-open for someone to see. I highly believe in the level of its functionality and degree of outcomes.

Additionally, the magnitude of accomplishments from this club is worth sharing with you before you start your dream business.

## A dedicated restaurant club becomes a millionaire club

Please allow me to change the mindset of you and your club members just a little bit, from the ordinary to the millionaire. You need to elevate your thinking ability to one that is capable of performing major successful projects. The idea is for you to stop deciding to start a restaurant for granted. Start thinking big and trust your gut. Believe that you can start a business with the ability to generate millions of dollars ahead.

From now on, I prefer this club to be called a millionaire club because it magnifies your vision and helps you visualize this world from a different angle. From this angle, there are many positive characteristics, such as:

- Being unstoppable no matter the circumstances.
- Understanding problems should be called challenges.
- Understanding the availability of various sources of finance to support your business.
- Self-motivation.

- Having big, collective, and attainable visions that are reviewed periodically and amended to fit the current and future needs of the business.
- Understand the importance of everyone around you and utilizing their talents for a win-win atmosphere.

Having a millionaire mindset is the same as having a new arsenal that will maximize your ability to attain your business goals in a given time frame. You need to understand that almost all millionaires and billionaires start small. But their mindsets are what make the difference between them winning or losing.

## Why is it called a Millionaire Club?

It is a club with the main goal of changing your *mindset* from an **ordinary mindset** to a **millionaire mindset.** As you start preparing to enter this club, it is the right moment for you to:

- Get out of your comfort zone.
- Be ready to start facing challenges that help you to grow up.
- Start thinking big.
- Empower yourself with functional and productive thoughts.
- Have friends who uplift you.
- Believe in yourself and say, "**YES,** you can do it."

That is what the millionaire club is all about; changing the financial outlook of your life for good!

# What is a millionaire mindset?

The millionaire mindset is a way of thinking that opens your thinking ability to the one that relies on something greater than what you feel right now. It is a kind of feeling that gives you the courage to overcome the fear and challenges ahead. Moreover, it empowers you to achieve financial success much sooner than others with ordinary mindsets. If you want to be a millionaire, you need to learn how to think, act, and feel like a millionaire. Opening a restaurant business is a great move that has all three elements in one—thinking, acting, and feeling like a millionaire.

# What is the personality of a millionaire?

Millionaires are **creative visionaries with a positive attitude**. In other words, wealthy people have big dreams, and they believe they will come true. As such, wealth seekers should set lofty goals and not be afraid of uncharted territory.

**Specific mindsets about wealth that all millionaires share.**

Unless you are ready to push a button in your brain from ordinary to wealthy, the efforts of reading this book will not help you much. Thinking and doing things at a low level as you have been doing in the past has to change. Try to adopt a new way of looking at this world, especially from a financial point of view.

Below are the mindsets of millionaires:

- **Not viewing failure as a failure:** Making a mistake and learning through mistakes is a part of the game when seeking success. Do not be afraid to try and fail when investing in a business. A lot of successful people learn from their failures while climbing the ladder of wealth.

- **Let others work for you:** People with a millionaire mindset are always looking for effective ways to delegate responsibilities to reproduce their success or enhance their achievements. Expect to hire employees to work on your restaurant to help you build your fortune one brick at a time.

- **Making more money:** Millionaires focus on making more money rather than saving. Tirelessly, they keep reinvesting any excess income they make for more returns down the road.

- **No room for giving up:** They do not believe in failure as the end of their efforts to achieve their goals. They learn through mistakes and keep moving forward.

- **Dream big:** Millionaires always strive to move out of their comfort zones to accomplish extraordinary goals.

- **Possession of empowering mindsets:** They have empowering mindsets about wealth. They believe it is possible to get there. To attain this goal, they have comprehensive plans that are functional and achievable within a reasonable timeframe.

- **Holding their destiny:** They believe they are capable of creating and owning their destiny.

- **Being responsible for personal failure:** They take responsibility for their results no matter how bad they are. Once they accept and own their mistakes, they find positive measures of overcoming them and making sure they will not happen again.

- **Play safe is not the option:** Millionaires understand that getting out of their comfort zone creates challenges. The challenges can only be dominated when they accept that there is a chance of failure outside of their will; while looking for solutions.

- **Presence of many fortunes:** They always know and believe that prosperity is abundant on the playing field. It is just a matter of getting inside and looking around.

- **High level of curiosity:** Millionaires are opportunity seekers. They possess an open-minded mentality that helps them spot a good deal in a matter of seconds.

- **They are surrounded by smart people:** If you stop sharpening your knife, there is a point it will stop cutting as fast as it used to cut before. Millionaires are constantly applying this concept in their lives by exploring new ideas from smart people for their benefit.

- **They rarely eat along**: The word eats has been used as a general term. Generally, the point is, millionaires, know how to open the doors in their networks for productive and smart people. They constantly need manpower to help them push their agenda faster and productively. You can do the same by opening your millionaire club. The process is simple. Take a look at the procedures below.

More than ever, it is time to shake things up and understand the need for adopting the "millionaire mindset." Adopt a new way of thinking that can change your fortune, future, and business. Work to achieve the financial success that others failed to accomplish.

# ◀))))Attention

There are many informal millionaire and billionaire clubs in the country. However, they are hard to allocate or to be admitted once you earmark one. However, you do not need to spend valuable time and money looking for them. You can start your club in a few days or weeks. If you do the homework right, it can be as functional and attractive as possible.

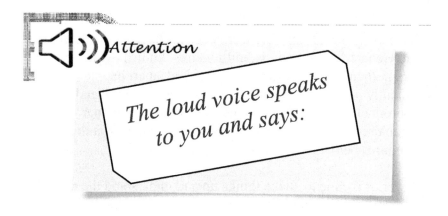

◀)))Attention

The loud voice speaks to you and says:

## This is the right moment!

## Start your own

## Millionaire Club right now!

# Formation of Millionaire Club

I do not believe you want to be just an ordinary business owner!

One who is making a small amount of money to meet only basic end needs. I am highly certain you want to join this business arena with bold and attainable visions of changing your financial life for good. You want to build a business that is making a decent profit, higher than what you are making on your current job. The millionaire club helps you attain these goals much faster with less stress. It is a short-cut route majority of successful people have been using as a competitive factor against their rivals. Without a doubt, while preparing to enter this business arena, it will be a wise idea to start preparing the road map of forming this club right away.

Running a successful restaurant business works better when you form *a team of the most aggressive and ambitious participants*. No matter the geographical location, the members of this group can be located in any city within the United States. It does not matter. You can include in your list coworkers, relatives, friends, and neighbors.

## Primary characteristics

Below are the characteristics of this winning syndicated team:

- Choose only people you trust and are willing to share information freely.
- Aim for all of you to become business owners when necessary.
- Proximity should not be an issue. No matter the geographical location, you can have some members living in other cities.
- This is not a club for raising capital; it is for running the business together. Sharing working capital should be an optional decision rather than mandatory. If a few of you want to form a partnership that includes sharing working capital, that is fine. However, do not expel other members who do not wish to become partners.

- Make sure your team is dependable and shares the same purpose, especially in difficult times.
- You need cheerleaders around you rather than idea crushers. When surrounded by motivational friends, it helps to get the additional energy you need to keep pursuing your goals no matter the circumstances.
- You need business-minded team members. When you speak to them, just about every conversation should be about business.
- Try to make sure all members are equal in terms of decision-making. When necessary, avoid having classes of participants since this is just a small club and not a business partnership.

## Club Objectives

This club belongs to all of you, which gives you the ability to add or reduce the general objectives of forming the group. In the beginning, utilize the purpose indicated below while generating more functional objectives that suit your needs.

The primary goals of the millionaire club are:

- **Raising working capital:** You do not have to raise capital like partners. Instead, give each other tips or ideas for allocating cheap and convenient sources of funds. For instance, assume you know a community bank in your city that offers loans to small business owners at lower rates and less strict requirements. In the business world, it is considered valuable information needs to be passed on to all club members. The same applies if you know financial institutions that issue credit cards with great benefits for the cardholders. Yes, this is the kind of information your colleagues need to know right away.

- **Locating new talents**: Generally, running a successful restaurant depends on having sizeable dedicated and experienced employees. In the labor shortage market, it is hard to find good employees without emptying your savings. However, with the help of club members, the process of recruiting the right people can be much easy and saves time.

- **Sharing responsibilities:** Combining members with various backgrounds helps to open the door for many talents and experiences with less stress. Likewise, the money needed to recruit these talents will not be there, which is another big advantage for all club members. Assume you have five members in your millionaire club including yourself, the first one is an accountant (CPA). You can see that you do not need to hire an accountant because you have a CPA within the group. Even if you pay the person, the fees will be much less compared with outsourcing the same task to a stranger. The more talented members in your club, the better it is for your business. The cost of allocating a few missing talents from your club is lower compared to hiring all the essential talented people needed to run your business.

- **Sharing stress:** We all want to hear good news all the time; instead of receiving stressful information every single minute. Unfortunately, strangers or outsiders never fall in the category of dependable people to ask for free professional advice or comfort news when you need it most.

However, having dedicated members in your club can provide valuable advice at the right time and free of charge. That is why the need for having enthusiastic club members is starting to shine.

**General Views:**

- I want you to be the main supporter of this wonderful idea. The awareness of becoming one of the millionaires and start enjoying the American dream in your lifetime.
- The truth is, having a *Millionaire Club* helps a lot in overcoming daily business challenges that can be a little harder to resolve by yourself.
- Do not worry, the fortunes of this industry are many and you cannot finish them yourself.
- The food industry is one of the biggest industries and it keeps growing each year. The bigger the cities are becoming, the higher the opportunities are growing to open another restaurant.

# How to get participants on board?

It is simple like A, B, C!

Bold business-minded people are unstoppable no matter the challenges they face. So do you!

## Step One

- Start by developing a contact list. Us the chat below as a starting point. You can modify it to suit your desires.
- You need at least ten people on your contact list.
- Contact them and explain the idea of becoming club members or business owners. For those who want to form a partnership, give them a chance to go in that route.
- When possible, create a discussion group on social media to simplify communications among participants. Besides, it helps to get a lot of positive responses.

## Sample: Contact Form

| Name | Contact Info | Yes Response | No Response |
|---|---|---|---|
| Relatives | | | |
| Friends | | | |
| Co-workers | | | |
| Neighbors | | | |

**Step Two**

- Develop a second list out of the first list and call it, let's say "decliner". It includes those with **"NO"** and **"Maybe"** responses.
- You may consider adding new members when necessary.
- If your tactics of persuasion have run short for encouraging them to join the club; then, change your convincing tune. Try to influence them to read this book or attend industrial seminars. The advantages of reading a book are better than getting information from other sources. Some of the benefits are:

  - **Low price:** Books are much cheaper than attending seminars.
  - **Convenient:** Reading a book can be done at any time without interrupting your schedule.
  - **More contents:** It holds a lot of well-written and edited information that cannot be covered in three hours or a one-day seminar.

- **Source of reference:** Books allow you to have a remote discussion. It is just a matter of selecting a page and getting exactly what you want to explore. It facilitates being on the same page with other team members.
- Allow the participants to ask you questions after they read the book in an attempt of maximizing the **"YES"** response.
- Then conduct a second roll call.

**Step Three**

- The goal is to have at least four **"Yes"** responses.
- At this point of brainstorming, I believe you and your team members will all be on board ready to explore more indispensable information to start your businesses soon.
- Make social media discussion groups active and vibrant. Possibly, modify or add more discussion groups in other media to meet the needs of all members.

**Step Four**

Prepare a contact list. Utilize the chart below as a starting point.

## Sample: Millionaire Club Contact List

| # | Name | Position | Phone Number | Email Address | Others |
|---|------|----------|--------------|---------------|--------|
| 1 | | President | | | |
| 2 | | Secretary | | | |
| 3 | | Member | | | |
| 4 | | Member | | | |
| 5 | | Member | | | |
| 6 | | Member | | | |
| 7 | | Member | | | |
| 8 | | Member | | | |
| 9 | | Member | | | |
| 10 | | Member | | | |

## Step Five

Develop the final inclusive list that shows all major characteristics within one page.

## Name: .......................Millionaire Club

## List of Active Member

| # | Name | Position | Professional | Preferred Contact | Location | Active/Non-Active |
|---|------|----------|--------------|-------------------|----------|-------------------|
| 1 | | President | | | | |
| 2 | | Secretary | | | | |
| 3 | | Member | | | | |
| 4 | | Member | | | | |
| 5 | | Member | | | | |
| 6 | | Member | | | | |
| 7 | | Member | | | | |
| 8 | | Member | | | | |
| 9 | | Member | | | | |
| 10 | | Member | | | | |

# How to run the millionaire club

Below are some of the techniques for operating your club:
- Since the concept of sharing the working capital is not on the table, there is no need for having a treasurer. However, the club should leave that decision to its members who want to form a partnership.
- Based on the nature and size of the club, no formal registration is needed. However, once it starts to allow contributions to come or the number of members increases, one may consider making it formal by registering it in the state of your choice.
- Formation of a club of this nature allows having members from any state. Productivity will be maximized when you create a simple but functional means of communication.
- You can create an informal bylaw when necessary.
- Make sure you set attainable and productive goals that will attract more members to join in. Moreover, it will help to maximize the retention rate. Some of the restaurant-related goals are shown below:

    - Share detailed business deals available in each other towns or states.
    - Discuss the possibilities of accommodating each other when a member decides to open a restaurant outside of their hometown.
    - Try to discuss various techniques for selecting key players (mentors, accountants, and loan managers).
    - Explore nice, profitable sections in the city where you can open a restaurant.
    - Discuss available permits and other limitations in your area and how to overcome them much faster with less stress.
    - Share the list of experienced, punctual, and cheap contractors located within a reasonable distance. It helps if you will lease a building that needs repair work.

- Consider various options when looking for bargains. As you find more and more ways to save money, share that information with all club members.
- Help each other choose target customers. Strive to select the right customers who match the characteristics of your business model.
- Do not forget to celebrate any win that is happening among club members. It can be celebrated by:
  - Having lunch or dinner.
  - Going to play golf.
  - Going fishing, etc.
- Utilize these gatherings to share things such as:
  - Refocus on your primary goals.
  - Look after past mistakes and find permanent solutions for the benefit of all members.
  - Reset goals when necessary.
  - Discuss the idea of tackling bigger projects when deemed essential.

You may add additional productive topics to your discussions. However, try to focus on the current business model until you get enough experience. From there, you may consider jumping into tougher projects.

The millionaire club discussion indicates that the benefits of starting these clubs are far better than doing nothing. Consider opening your club much sooner to start utilizing the advantages of sharing expertise with other members. The benefits of having these members are greater when compared with the threats of them being your immediate competitors. Members can also live outside of your hometown or on another side of the city limit. If some of your members want to open a restaurant, you can target the middle class while others focus on the lower-income group or upper class. Alternatively, you can divide the market using subdivisions such as east, west, south, and north or cities available in a big city. The bottom line is that doing nothing is not an option.

# Important Take Away Memorandum

This is a *very important chapter* that carries much weight in this book.

It facilitates your dreams of becoming a successful business owner to happen much soon compare with your competitors.

The chapter is worth reading <u>*more than once*</u> to retain a full understanding of the message.

I highly suggest starting your Millionaire Business Club right away ahead of your rivals.

Once the message and the actions of starting this club are met:

Then,

The full purpose of investing in this book will be reached much quicker.

Moreover,

The goal of the writer will be met as well.

# To-Do List Form – Chapter Two

| Action | Goals | Results(Y/N) |
|---|---|---|
| Time-sensitive actions:<br><br>1.<br><br>2.<br><br>3.<br><br>4.<br><br>5.<br><br>6.<br><br>7.<br><br>8.<br><br>9.<br><br>10. | | |
| Less time-sensitive actions<br><br>1.<br><br>2.<br><br>3.<br><br>4. | | |

| | | |
|---|---|---|
| 5. | | |
| 6. | | |
| 7. | | |
| 8. | | |
| 9. | | |
| 10. | | |

# Read Again Pages – Chapter Two

| Page # | Topic/Subtopic | Purpose | Result (Y/N) |
|---|---|---|---|
|  |  |  |  |
|  |  |  |  |
|  |  |  |  |
|  |  |  |  |
|  |  |  |  |

# Chapter Three

## Building the foundation of your business

This chapter exposes a roadmap you need while preparing yourself to move into this arena. Starting any new project, assignment, job, or business needs a compass that tells you:

- what tasks to complete
- how to complete the tasks
- a target date for completing the tasks

Starting a successful business requires the same discipline of readiness. Expect to learn and practically be able to utilize a winning equation in your daily business operations. Running a successful business requires preparing a comprehensive business plan. All procedures of preparing it are well demonstrated without forgetting the types of business formations and procedures of opening a business account. You will learn how to register your business and find a location to rent. Starting a restaurant is so easy with the help of the invaluable information supplied in this chapter.

The process of generating satisfactory profit can be done very easily with the help of the winning equation. Let us unfold the equation in a detailed manner as shown in the next page:

# Winning equation

**Winning equation**

=

**Profound Logic + Tremendous Creativity + Critical Thinking**

# Profound logic

## Definition of the word logic

According to the Oxford University Dictionary, the definition of logic is (1) a: the science of reasoning, proof, thinking, or inference. (c) Ability in reasoning. Oxford University Press, pg. 583.

As you move forward with preparing to start a business, you must understand that a closer look at every decision you plan to execute is essential. Be sure to apply a high degree of logic when making decisions. Each decision has to meet the so-called **why, how, and when benchmarks.** Start by asking yourself **why** you want to do something. For example, let's say you decided to put tiles in the sitting room rather than wood or carpet. The next step is **how** are you going to do it? Also, **why** choose that route? Lastly, **when** do you want to do it?

The point of these questions is to help you focus your attention on the action you want to accomplish. Because you need time and money to initiate any project, you better think deeply about the reasons behind your actions. You will constantly be advised to focus on adding value to your property or project. Meanwhile, avoid tackling projects that waste money even though they make you feel comfortable. The main idea here is that you are entering into a business arena to make money, not to please your feelings. For instance, replacing a kitchen in restaurant "A," can be a waste of money than in restaurant "B". This example will make sense only if you create a habit of utilizing a high degree of logic in all decisions relating to your daily business operations.

# Tremendous creativity

## Definition of a word creativity

According to *Human Motivation*, 3rd ed., by Robert E. Franken: defined the word creativity is the tendency to generate or recognize ideas, alternatives, or possibilities that may be useful in solving problems, communicating with others, and entertaining ourselves and others. Thinking beyond a box continues to be the norm in any for-profit organization when there is a primary goal of maximizing ROI in a particular period.

For instance, adding a wall or removing a wall between a dining room and a kitchen will cost a little extra money from your budget. In addition to adding a good looking to your restaurant, the proper execution of the project might make the building look brighter and better. In return, customers will be willing to keep coming to eat in your restaurant rather than going to your competitors. Going the extra mile beyond ordinary business owners is a rule of thumb for ambitious operators who want to make an extra profit.

Remember, all the essential knowledge you need to run a successful business is at your fingertips. Just try to utilize your resources and time effectively through learning by reading books, attending seminars, seeking help from a mentor, or getting advice from professionals when necessary.

# Critical thinking

## Definition of critical thinking

According to Michael Scriven and Richard Paul (2003) also adopted by the University of Louisville, they defined critical thinking is the intellectually disciplined process of actively and skillfully conceptualizing, applying, analyzing, synthesizing, and/or evaluating information gathered from, or generated by, observation, experience, reflection, reasoning, or communication, as a guide to belief and action.

Although logical and critical thinking is somehow the same, there is a slight difference between the two terms worth exploring. Critical thinking is a process of evaluation that uses logic to separate truth from falsehood, reasonable from unreasonable beliefs. Since critical thinking helps you separate truth from falsehood or the reasonable from the unreasonable, you can see how essential a high level of critical thinking is in running any successful business.

For instance, many states' food and safety rules require the restaurant owner to seek a permit before starting a restaurant. It does not matter how much it costs, how long it takes, or how cumbersome the procedure is when securing a permit. Ultimately, it is worth taking the long route and waiting for permission from the city. When you get caught by city personnel, the consequences are harsh, more severe, and will jeopardize the stability of your business.

No matter who tries to convince you to choose inappropriate ways of cutting corners, use your intellect to prevent falling into that trap. When the dust settles, you will be in trouble and in a position of losing money, not the third party. The same scenario might happen when you are renovating your new building for your restaurant business. You might have to seek some permits before start working on the project. The bad news is that there are a lot of bad contractors in the field who take advantage of inexperienced business owners to cut corners here and there. They want to get quick money and move to the next project without remorse for the homeowners. So be careful not to be the next person in the line. Protect yourself by using common sense for every piece of action that is happening with your projects. The money you save helps maximize profit in your business.

All three components of the winning equation should be applied together to produce full results in your venture. The process has to be done regardless of the size, duration, budget, or location of the project. One might ask, out of these three which component is more important than the other? The correct answer is that they all are equally as important. The type of project that you are applying can be a prime determinant without forgetting your degree of understanding and the capability of utilizing these components in the real world.

Do not worry that you may not be a good thinker, that you cannot logically execute most actions, or that your level of thinking is not sharp enough. Lack of competency can be overcome once you adopt a habit of learning new things promptly. Do not be shy to ask questions or clarification in your areas of weakness. There is no single person in this universe who knows everything.

🔊Attention

Starting a restaurant business involves a lot of money and efforts that make some participants be defensive or offended when you approach them in sensitive areas of their businesses. To break this barrier in your favor, you have to apply a high level of professionalism and charisma while presenting yourself in front of the potential knowledge holders.

# The right time to start your business

There is no better time to join a restaurant business than now. One might ask a sounding question, why is this the right moment to become a business owner when I am a newcomer with no business background or experience?

The excitement of starting a business differs from one person to another. It depends on many factors, such as the degree of readiness, the level of preparations, and the current market situation, just to name a few. The more you prepare yourself, the more confident you will be when it is time to take the first step in the restaurant business. It is commonly known that if you want to get an "A" on your exam, you have to start by setting a functional roadmap of how to achieve the goal. The same concept is applicable in the business arena.

If you want to start a profitable business, make sure you map out every detail and actively work on manifesting those goals. Deeply, look at direct and indirect factors that might contribute to or derail business operations and try to find ways of overcoming them. Attempt to find solutions for all challenges before you start your business. Failure to search and employ functional solutions will gradually cause your business to deteriorate or dissolves completely. Below are areas you need to be familiar with while preparing to lunch your business:

## Personal characters

Just because your coworker or a close friend started a successful business does not mean that your business will be an overnight success. Running a sound business requires a lot of preparations and commitments that most people find it is too much for them to pursue this route. As a result, they crush the idea and continue to become employees again.

When starting a business, it is common to see owners working more than eight hours a day, including weekends. This is a new working style that you might encounter in your business; it needs quick adoption with a full level of participation. You have to start by adjusting your lifestyle. Sometimes these adjustments might flow to your family members. In other words, try to incorporate them into your idea of becoming a business owner and make sure all of you are on the same page to avoid a surprise down the road. Carefully listen to their opinions by opening up your body language, staying engaged, not interrupting, and asking questions to ensure everyone is on the same page. Leave room for compromise when necessary with the new schedule you present to them. Seek their approval ahead of time to avoid any form of rebellion in the future.

Once all family members, if applicable, are on board with your ideas, then you can go ahead and move to the next step of assessing your level of readiness. Start by evaluating how ready you are to become a successful business owner with the consideration of many aspects of your life structure. List down all essential characters that you think might affect your business directly or indirectly. Then make two lists:

- **List one:** It comprises all strengths you bring to the business.
- **List two:** It includes weaknesses that you think might need immediate correction if your business begins to derail.

Take one weakness at a time and find ways of making sure they do not become a heavy burden to carry while running your venture. For example, if you are not strong enough to discipline someone in real-time, try to overcome this trait before becoming a new chief executive officer (CEO).

You do not want to be seen as a boss just by name or title alone; meanwhile, you cannot meet many functions associated with this position. Try joining many professional organizations such as the Chamber of Commerce, professional development training, or researching literature geared towards helping you develop managerial, finance, and accounting skills.

Also, take the initiative to seek a mentor willing to work with you in many aspects of your business operations in real-time. Make sure you pick a person who is reliable, experienced, and sometimes if not always – the one who shares the same characteristics with yours. The odds of finding a good mentor are slim. However, when you find one, use them to your advantage. The chance of gaining positive results in your business when having a mentor is much higher compared to operating without one. Attend seminars and exchange contact information with other attendees. Be intentional and express your purpose for seeking a mentor. Building a relationship with your mentor may take time. Looking for someone to guide you in business operations can be time-consuming.

However, when you do find a mentor, please be sure to value their knowledge, as well as their time. Also, don't be afraid to barter. Offer to take your mentor to lunch, pay for their gas, or a taxi in exchange for their valuable insight. If you know of anything that can help them enhance their business, share that information as well. Let that be your way of showing gratitude.

Another option of having a mentor to guide you while starting your business is to hire a professional. It is sad to see that most prospects are willing to start a business with, let's say, $130,000. Meanwhile, they are not willing to hire an expert to guide them in this process. It depends on the scope of work and location. The professional fee might start at as little as $2,000. You need someone around you who is well experienced and willing to offer essential information and the necessary guidance to help you start a successful business. I think it is worth spending a few dollars before or during the initial stages of business operations to kill two birds at once.

First, you want to protect the money you worked hard saving over several years. Secondly, you also want to see your dream of becoming a successful business owner reached sooner than later. Now here is a very important question. Why are most prospects and sometimes existing business owners not ready to spend $2,000 to protect $128,000? This is a million-dollar question most business consultants like me never stop asking. Caution: fully utilize your wisdom (winning equation) to avoid falling into the same trap many are experiencing. It is an avoidable and unnecessary deception that most prospects and business owners take for granted before finding themselves losing money in a matter of a short time.

# Vision and Mission Statement

A vision statement is a directional path that shows you how to reach the final destination. It is a business road map indicating all necessary guidelines the company should undertake, including setting an expanded target of growth for the business.

# 🔊 Attention

*A business vision statement to be functional* must align with its mission, strategic planning, culture, and core values.

## Components of the vision statement

The vision statement is imperative in shaping the goals and direction of the company and helps maximize the return on investment. Below is a list of key components of the mission statement:

a. It analyzes the future prime of the state of the company. It reveals the primary things the organization is planning to achieve in a given time frame.
b. The vision statement offers guidance and inspiration on the action the business is planning to accomplish.

# Mission statement

A mission statement is a short comprehensive proclamation describing a company's primary purpose. Although companies aim to make them permanent, they change as a company grows and adopts new objectives, replacing the old ones.

## 🔊 Attention

*The mission statement* supports the vision and serves to communicate purpose and direction to employees, customers, vendors, and other stakeholders.

A functional and inclusive mission statement comprises the following characteristics:

- The mission statement should define the main goals of the company.
- It should describe what the company desires to be within three, five, ten, or twenty years.
- Also, it should be limited to distinguish other ventures but broad enough to allow for creative growth.
- The mission statement should be broad and serve as a framework for evaluating the company's performance.
- The mission statement should reveal all the primary goals of the company.
- It should clearly and broadly analyze the steps of attaining the projected goals.
- It should guide the company's executive decisions (decision-making process).

**Components of Mission Statement**

There are three primary elements of the mission statement shown below:

- **Key market:** Pinpoint the target market. Clearly, assess your market and its primary characteristics.
- **Contribution:** Clearly and broadly analyze what products you offer to the clients. Anytime you change the types of food you offer, you need to refresh your mission statement as well.
- **Distinction:** Clearly, express your market niche. Communicate the level of food you want to sell or unique service, compared to your rivals, in a clear and precise manner.

🔊))Attention

Do not confuse the difference between a mission statement and a vision statement.

## Difference between mission and vision statements

| Mission statement | Vision statement |
|---|---|
| • It deals with the "cause." | • It deals with "effect." |
| • It reveals what you must accomplish. | • It deals with things to be done to meet intended accomplishments. |
| • It answers the "why" question. | • It answers the "what" question. |
| • The primary purpose is to inform. | • The primary purpose is to inspire. |
| • It majors in doing activities. | • It majors in seeing activities. |
| • It offers a general idea of how to achieve the vision. | • It unfolds a big picture of things to be completed. |
| • It guides you on how to arrive safely at the final destination. | • If presents to you the destination of the company. |

## Core Values

A core value represents the basic elements that are guiding the way we execute our work. They are our business's fundamental driving force and carry the foremost priorities of what to be done daily. These statements comprise general company rules and values required to form functional and productive culture. Examples of core values are highlighted below:

a. Establish and practice state-of-the-art total quality management.
b. Focus on a new functional and productive business culture.
c. Focus on and improve innovative customer service.
d. Establish an up-to-date and efficient logistic system.

# Strategies

A strategy is a tactical plan of action the managerial team is executing to attain company goals. For instance, the team might decide to set marketing strategies such as developing new ads and hiring an additional sales task force to boost sales by 1 million in the next six months. Strategies play a major role in maximizing a company's success because they are a starting point for formulating plans for accomplishing tasks. Indeed, the more specialized your business is, the higher the need for creativity in coming up with inclusive business strategies.

# Goals

Goals are a group of general statements explaining the tasks required to implement a strategy. Examples of company goals are listed below:

a. Decrease food waste
b. Improve sales
c. Change package design for the takeaway foods
d. Improve public relation
e. Improve teamwork

Make sure your business goals align with the general purposes of executing the strategy. To avoid over-utilizing the business resources or losing the primary focus, avoid planning excessively many goals. Try to avoid any interference and contradiction that might occur while implementing your goals; make sure you set accurate and organized goals.

# ◁))) Attention

Prepare the functional vision, mission, core values, strategies, and goals of your business with precision. This road map is significant in guiding your daily business operations and ensuring the execution and success of meeting short and long-term goals.

# Business plan

A business plan is an essential written document that provides a description and overview of your company's future. All businesses should have a business plan, no matter the size of the business. The plan should explain your business strategy and your key goals to get from where you are now to where you want to be in the future. It carries your visions from where you are momentarily and draws a road map of where you want to be in a given time period. When written properly, it gives you an idea of what is supposed to happen, why it is happening, and how it is happening now, not yesterday and not tomorrow.

Since a business plan carries your business ideas or visions, it must be confidential. Mainly to avoid your unfaithful friends or relatives from sharing or claiming your ideas as their own. Here you can see the need of having only trustworthy members in your winning club to preserve your business ideas.

A comprehensive Business plan saves your business and carries three important purposes if it is well-written. Below are the major purposes of the business plan:

- **It creates effective business growth strategies in real-time:** A good business plan analyzes all essential steps for the business to undertake while operating, including techniques of dealing with vendors, employees, and debtors, without forgetting how to overcome the challenges of competitors. Therefore, it plays a major role in acting as a GPS while driving a car showing you when to take a certain action, where that action leads your business, and at what cost. It is a very important document to new and existing business owners, regardless of the company size. More importantly, it needs to be revised gradually depending on the economic or political changes happening while running your business. You want to have a document that carries the current status of the business environment in which your company is positioned. That way, you will have peace of mind knowing the chance of hitting positive ROI is much higher.

- **It analyses future financial needs of the business:** Running a successful restaurant business also needs close attention to both inflow and outflow of money during business operations. You must have a solid projection indicating how much cash in hand you need right now, a month from now, this quarter, or for the entire year. Having too much cash in hand is as bad as not having enough cash to meet the daily demands of business operations, such as paying vendors, purchasing inventories, or covering payroll expenses. Once you prepare a detailed budget that accommodates the financial statement section, you can identify the right amount of working capital needed for a given period.

The idea of having a detailed budget handy facilitates understanding how much cash you need in the next quarter or any stated time period. In case of any cash shortage, the ample time you have can help you develop ideas ahead of time to secure the additional cash you need. The same is true when expecting more cash than you need to cover business operations. Then you can consider various options of investing it to generate more money instead of it sitting in your bank account earning little to no interest.

- **It is a machine tool to attract investors:** Serious investors know how to research promising businesses to invest in for long-term benefits. One of the tools they use to find companies to purchase or invest in is business plans. All indications are there to tell you that a business plan is not just a document like other regular documents. It is a backbone of your business that saves well to meet major business operations both internally and externally.

If you are planning to seek external help, try to pick an experienced person in this field. Select someone who will be able to go through market trends, research reports, and other current materials that analyze in detail the past, current, and future position of the restaurant industry. In the end, you want to have at your disposal a solid document broad enough to explain each step of running a profitable business. The well-written business plan should cover all essential components as indicated below:

**Executive summary:** This section comprises a general overview of your business. It indicates what you want to do and how you want to do it, and the purposes of starting your venture now and not tomorrow. Make sure also to include the following components in this section:

- **Mission statement of your business:** Mission statement entails the major objectives behind the general purpose of starting your business. Also, it explains fundamental approaches to meet the stated objectives.

- **Product/service summary**: Briefly explain how the restaurant business you want to start is different from your competitors.

- **Market opportunity summary:** In this segment, you need to indicate what market niche your business will fit in. Copying and pasting what others/competitors are doing is not a business strategy and will not guarantee or affirm the future existence of your business.

  Use the winning equation above to see what problem your *competitors* are missing before developing bold strategies for fulfilling them.

- **Traction summary:** If there are any fundamental accomplishments you manifested in the past that you think will play a major role in reshaping your new venture, then use this section to analyze them. Try to be as specific as possible and use examples when applicable to support your points.

- **Milestones summary:** Precisely and in summary form, explain what objectives you want to accomplish in a given time frame. For instance, in the next nine months, you want to a second restaurant or, within one year, you will stop leasing a van and purchase yours.

- **Vision statement:** Explain the big picture of your business. How does that look? Be exact when stating what you want to accomplish as a business owner and why you will do it. Address the problem you want to solve in society and how you plan to solve it. If there is no West African restaurant in Dallas and you want to start one, explain that point in your vision statement section. A vision statement carries a future flag of your business. In return, the elements of Mission and Vision Statements work together to join the company's purposes, goals, and values.

**Business description:** This section provides room to explain in detail the general purposes of starting your business and the problem you want to solve. Do not take the information in this section lightly when analyzing this section. This section carries important information most investors, bankers, and other external creditors want to review while judging the creditability of your business. All problems you plan to solve should be analyzed one at a time, along with the corresponding detailed solutions your business plans to deliver. While preparing this section, try to utilize these statements for guidance:

- Uncover the service you want to deliver to the market. In this case, it is selling food. But, you have to add more clarifications of how you will be selling your food, including other services you are planning to offer.
- Review all solutions available of what the restaurant business will solve in real-time.
- Make sure you state the positive outcomes of your solutions and how they impact the lives of customers.
- Focus on how your service will solve the existing problem for your customers.

**Market analysis:** Clearly, reveal the market niche of your service in the targeted market. This section needs full utilization of research data from credible sources to justify your claims. Use charts and pyramids to clarify and explain your outcomes when necessary. Since you need to have enough evidence of a solid market before the start of your business, make sure your analysis covers these major areas:

- **The size of the market:** In detailed form, indicate the degree of availability of customers in your target market. Be sure to allocate a sizeable group of customers who are willing to support your business. Possibly, try to find research data that indicates the existence of the market expansion. In return, the statistics will assure the future growth of your business.

- **The magnitude of market growth:** Consider analyzing the report in this order:
  - Make sure you mention the size of the market in your target area.
  - Record the projected annual revenue generated in this industry.
  - State whether your market is growing, stable, or slowing down.
  - If it is growing, show what the projected figure will look like in the next five, ten, or fifteen years from now.

- **Fundamental trends that drive your market niche:** Try to pinpoint the presence of new behavior, the idea that positively supports the market position of your business. For instance, most customers want to eat organic foods or meals that have been prepared in a clean environment.

- **Existence of positive outcomes from your competitors in the market:** Indicate how profitable existing businesses are in the industry. You need to show the existence of green pasture in the market that will benefit your business once you decide to start one.

- **Marketing and sales plan:** In this section, be specific and detailed about all techniques you plan to use to secure the market you service. In case you will rely on radio and TV ads, state that and the corresponding reasons for choosing these options.

**Competitive analysis:** This is a sensitive section of your business plan because your business will not be a monopoly in nature. It will operate in a heavily competitive environment that will require a high degree of professionalism to prevail. The rule of thumb is to execute each aspect of your business model. In return, your efforts will open the door to success much easier than you thought. Do not be afraid of anything. As always, help is around us all the time. It is just a matter of being creative and eager to look for it in real-time.

Advance to the next level by analyzing your primary competitors in your market, including their strengths and weaknesses. If done effectively, the list helps to indicate how to beat them in a specific aspect of their business operations, such as having the ability to cook delicious foods. You need to see if there is a way to deliver better service than your rivals. If quality is a primary factor, can you offer high-quality meals in the market at a reasonable price?

**Management and organization description:** Articulate the type of management style you prefer to adopt and the supporting reasons behind your preference. Use charts to show the flow of managerial positions and chain of command to speed up the decision-making process. Also, to eliminate unnecessary confusion among employees. Think about the type of management styles you prefer to adopt in your company: commanding, visionary, affiliative, democratic, pacesetting, and coaching. State the reason behind your decision to select a particular style versus others.

**Product and services description:** Describe in detail the restaurant business you are planning to start. What type of restaurant and in which tier level are you planning to specialize? Are you going to perform all cooking work yourself, only using employees, or will you use a mix of both? What are the reasons behind your preferences? Are they financially visible both on your side as well as to investors?

**Challenges and risks:** Each business operates under the umbrella of challenges and obstacles that force management to work very carefully to overcome those challenges for the betterment of the business. Set enough time to explore all challenges and risks you think you may encounter and record them. Make a comprehensive list of solutions for each one and their corresponding implementation timeframe. For instance, what will happen when your vendor increases the price of food and other supplies? What will you do to stay afloat? Consider developing not only a list of one solution per each challenge but multiple choices or remedies for each problem. Then, if plan "A" does not work, you can go to plan "B."

**Revenue projections:** Having a steady structure that ensures a constant flow of revenue enough to meet daily business operations is very important to overcome unnecessary destructions of business operations. The aftermath of the interruption might reduce the projected margin. As a manager, make sure you have a meticulous way of monitoring your business revenue projections and dependable sources of finances when you need them.

Since the option of not having a business plan in your business does not exist, then have a solid and functional plan before you start your business. It has to be inclusive of all essential information needed to meet the demand of the business you are about to start and the requirements of all shareholders. The plan holds important information regarding your business, so it always has to be secured. Periodically, monitor the status of its functionality. Perform necessary adjustments to suit the current requirements to keep generating projected revenue and ROI.

# Determine the legal structure of your business

When you decide to become a business owner, the next step is very important. You will be required to select the form of the business entity that is preferable to start. Certainly, your business depends on the business plan to secure starting capital if cash is not the first option. In addition to facilitating daily business operations, preparation of a comprehensive plan is met when you select the type of venture to start. You are required to know ahead of time whether you will operate your business as a sole proprietorship or with the collaboration of outsiders. Specifically, even if you want any form of partnership, you still need to narrow down your selection by establishing a limited liability company or corporation.

However, the process of coming up with a final and acceptable form of business is not easy and requires close attention to avoid roadblocks down the road. One of the primary objectives of entering the business arena is to open and successfully operate a business free of legal limbo or any other kind of obstacles. For these factors to be true, a lot of actions should be taken into consideration with the help of direct and indirect factors. Ironically, a good number of fundamental factors that play a direct role in influencing your decision process are indicated below:

- **Number of employees:** Assume you are planning to start a big business with many employees and a good number of branches; starting with a sole proprietorship or Limited Liability Company may not be preferable. Having a huge business idea like this works better when you start a C corporation.

- **Tax factor:** The federal government levies four basic types of business taxes: income tax, self-employment tax, taxes for employers, and excise taxes. As a business owner with no employees, do not worry about employee-related taxes; as compared to someone with workers. Employers, for instance, are required to pay another half of the total taxes relating to Social Security – 12.4 to15.3 percent and Medicare – 2.9 percent for the tax years 2021 and 2021. Also, a corporation (C Corporation) is subject to the double tax rule while other forms of business formation are not affected. So tax is a decisive factor. It plays a major influence when it is time to select what form of business to start. When necessary, you may consider seeking professional assistance from an attorney or accountant with a solid background in tax issues.

- **Size of business:** If one of your long-term plans is to have a big company with branches in many states, state that from the very beginning. Your tax professional will also analyze other factors before deciding the correct form of business to start.

- **Type of capital:** In case you plan to find a business partner to share the burden of business, automatically, the chance of starting a sole proprietorship entity will be eliminated. Additionally, if you plan to sell various types of shares in the future as a source of working capital; stating a corporation will be an ideal choice. Carefully, both short and long-term requirements of raising capital should be evaluated carefully to avoid legal problems in the future.

- **Degree of connection:** How much time you have and be willing to pour into your business may influence which business entity you prefer. The greater your desire to stay connected directly with your customers, the lesser the chance you have to establish a big company where you will hire employees to take your roles.

### Form of business entities

There are five forms of business entities for you to choose from and start a dream-restaurant business. Below is a list of business entities:

- Sole proprietorship
- Partnership
- Limited liability company (LLC)
- Corporation
    - C Corporation
    - S Corporation

## Sole Proprietorship

A sole proprietorship is one of the simplest forms of business structure that is preferable to most small business owners. The business will be entirely under your control, from executing registration activities to supervising daily operating activities. Ironically, there is no distinct line separating you from your business. You are a primary beneficiary of all business profits. As well as the sole person responsible when it comes time to bear business losses, debts, and other forms of business liabilities.

Legally, you are allowed to register your name as a business name. However, when you decide to come up with another name than your own, you will be asked to file what so-called *fictitious name*. It implies that your business is registered and operating with a designation other than your primary name. Moreover, the fictitious name also is known as a trading name and doing business as (DBA) name.

## Tax Obligations for Sole Proprietorship

The Internal revenue service (IRS) treats the sole proprietorship unit as an individual entity when paying taxes. As a self-employed or sole proprietorship, you are required to implement the following responsibilities to stay ahead of tax provisions:

- One obligatory is to file a tax return annually with no unnecessary excuses.
- You are obligated to participate in the quarterly estimated tax program. The payment periods and due dates are listed below:

### Payment of Estimated Tax

| Payment Period | Due Date |
|---|---|
| January 01 – March 31 | Payments should be done by April 15 |
| April 1 – May 31 | Payments should be done by June 15 |
| June 1 – August 31 | Payments should be done by September 15 |
| September 1 – December 31 | January 15 of the following year. |

🔊Attention

- If the due date for making an estimated tax payment falls on a Saturday, Sunday, or legal holiday, the payment will be approved on the next business day.

- Moreover, for more information on tax withholding and estimated tax, see Publication 505 of The Internal revenue service.

- You must pay se-employment tax (SE) together with income on due dates. Self-employment tax comprises Medicare as well as Social Security taxes. Use Form 1040-ES to perform combined tax estimation.
- You should use the standard Form 1040 in filing your tax return. Report all business income or losses in Schedule C.

**Advantages of a Sole Proprietorship**

As a sole proprietorship, you will experience many advantages that are not entitled to the other forms of business entities. Below is a list of primary benefits the sole proprietorship gets:

- **Easy tax preparation:** Compared with other forms of business entities, sole proprietorship has simple steps to complete while preparing an income tax return. You are required to prepare a separate business tax return. All business and personal information are combined in Form 1040, separated by schedules such as B, C, or D. For a restaurant owner, use schedule C.

- **Ample business control:** Having one hundred percent total control of your business is one of the factors most business owners prefer to join in this arena. It is the joy of running a business without worrying about pleasing someone else down the road. This option is not applicable in a partnership or when you have a large corporate entity.

- **Inexpensive to start:** Generally, it is so easy to start a sole proprietorship business compared to other forms of business entities. Lower legal costs for establishing a business, if deemed necessary, and simple financial statements are desirable.

- **Easy to meet personal goals:** Since not all prospects start businesses just for making a profit, sole proprietorship allows you to quickly attain other perks, such as freedom, flexibility, helping others, and being your own boss. A different number of objectives can be easily satisfied in conjunction with other supportive factors.

## Disadvantages of a sole proprietorship

Like other forms of business entities, sole proprietorship has some drawbacks that are important to consider before selecting this as your primary form of business to start. Below are disadvantages you may encounter as a business owner while operating under the umbrella of a sole proprietorship:

- **Raising capital:** Sole proprietorship business owners face a lot of roadblocks when it comes to raising working capital compared with other business entities. Legally, you cannot sell stocks as corporations do to get more money for meeting daily business operating expenditures. Moreover, lack of collateral may hinder your initiatives of seeking funds from financial institutions such as banks.

- **Unlimited personal liability:** Officially, there is no identifiable separation between you and your business. This type of legal situation makes you liable for all business liabilities, including any blunders that your workers might perform. Personal liability goes beyond business properties. Individual assets such as cars, houses, land, and furniture can be auctioned to cover business obligations.

- **Managerial deficiency:** As the business grows, many sole business owners experience an inability to control the pressure of daily business operations. If not controlled immediately, the problem might start to derail your business and diminish productivity. Moreover, hiring a competent employee might be too expensive for some new business owners to afford.

- **Working long hours:** In the beginning, the majority of sole business owners complain about working a lot. Some are having a difficult time getting weekends off. The fatigue coming from prolonged working hours might diminish the desire to be a business owner. And when this situation happens, it compromises the business. Long working hours also take family hours away. In most cases, it has been a major source of misunderstandings among couples to the point of triggering a divorce button.

# Partnership

A partnership occurs when two or more people join together to start a business entity. Each partner is obligated to contribute to the business in the form of money, assets, human capital, etc. Based on a partnership agreement, each partner is required to share business profits and losses. Before starting any business activities, a comprehensive agreement is established between all parties. They must analyze all major elements of daily business operations and be clear about each other's responsibilities. This covenant is called *a partnership agreement.*

## Partnership agreement

The partnership agreement is an official business contract binding all participants. In addition to helping daily business operations, it can also be used as a reference tool when things go wrong. The agreement is so useful when it is time for dissolving the business or when one partner is leaving the group willingly or unwillingly, in the case of death. To enforce its validity and usefulness, consider consulting an experienced attorney. Depending on the nature of the business you want to start, the partnership agreement should include all major elements that are not limited to:

- **Decision making:** It should identify major decisions and how they will be made.

- **Management:** Like other business entities, a partnership requires close attention to all aspects of business operations. Communicate the responsibility of each partner ahead of time to avoid confusion among yourselves and with employees. Establishing a clear chain of command corresponding with duties per participant is mandatory to maximize productivity so the business can operate smoothly.

- **Share of profits and losses:** The agreement should indicate how profits and losses will be shared among partners. Consider applying a fair method that will please all partners. One of the options is the percentage of capital contribution. Under this option, each partner will share profit or loss in the same proportion of the assets contributed to the venture. For example, you want to start a restaurant business with your two best friends. Assume friend A will bring $40,000 worth of assets, friend B will bring $35,000, and you will contribute $25,000. In percentage form, the contribution of each of you is a friend A: 40 percent, friend B: 35 percent, and yourself: 25 percent. When it is time to share profits and losses, you may use the same ratio to administer the division process. Logically, friend A has contributed a big chunk of assets compared with the two of you; in return, the person has a right to get a large share of either profit or loss you will make.

- **Resolve disputes:** The partnership agreement should state what procedures will be applied to settle disputes. Let it be inclusive as much as possible tackling all major issues existing in the restaurant industry.

- **Voting rights and responsibilities:** The outcome of any voting meeting has direct effects on daily business operations and you as an individual. Make sure the rights are inclusive and fair to all members. Clear remedies for the voting rights and primary duties should be stated and well enforced.

- **Change partnership:** If one or more partners are leaving, a proper plan has to be set in place showing all essential road maps to follow. The point is to protect the stability of the business and both parties. Protect the parties who are remaining and those who are ready to exit. This section also should include unexpected exits such as death.

- **Dissolution:** When the need arises to end the partnership, clear procedures should be stated to avoid unnecessary misunderstandings.

Regardless of the circumstances, do not start a business without a partnership agreement. Whether you are planning to start the business with a stranger, relative, friend, or acquaintance, let a contractual agreement lead the partnership. I have a lot of personal examples among others that reveal the complexity of running a business without having a comprehensive contract. Do not fall into this common trap. Depending only on legal interventions can be a painful journey you do not want to experience. In most cases, there is a higher chance of losing your claims since partners have the right to perform various duties without breaking the law. Statistically, a large number of people have lost a lot of money from sharing their valuable assets without proper protection. The idea of protecting your assets should prevail in your judgments while negotiating the contract deal.

## Types of Partnerships

Generally, there are three types of partnership arrangements:

- **General partnership:** A type of partnership agreement in which the partners are responsible for sharing all of the duties of daily business operations. Moreover, they are entitled to share profits and losses.

- **Limited partnership:** In this type of agreement, one general partner and other partners are considered limited partners. The general partner is the only one that must supervise all business operating activities. This person is responsible for both; compensation and sharing profit with other partners. Aside from sharing business losses with other partners (limited partners), the general partner is also answerable for other business obligations. Limited partners are not reliable on business debts beyond business losses.

- **Limited liability partnership:** Depending on the jurisdiction of your business location, all partners have limited liability status. Negligence or misconduct of one partner will not affect other partners. Limited liability means that if the partnership fails, then creditors cannot go after a partner's assets or income. Before opting for this category of the partnership agreement, conduct broad research to reveal the level of protection you are entitled to from unforeseeable events.

## ◁))) Attention

Consider seeking legal help when things start heating up. It is better to spend a few amounts of money on legal fees now, rather than spending a lot on resolving protectable problems in the future.

**Tax Obligations for Partnership**

To comply with rules and regulations, your business partnership should be legally registered and conform to all tax guidelines as shown below:

- **Tax ID number:** Your business should register with the IRS to get an employer identification number (EIN).
- **Annual information return:** On an annual basis, the business is required to reveal a report that shows various business operations such as:

  - total income made
  - all necessary deductions administered
  - the profits and losses of the business operations

- **Tax responsibilities:** Partners are individually responsible for the following taxes:
  - personal income tax
  - self-employment tax
  - estimated tax
  - Medicare and social security taxes
- **Tax form:** Partnerships should prepare and offer each partner Schedule K-1 and not W-2s. A single member is required to file an individual tax return using Form 1040, including Schedule C, the same as a sole proprietor.

As the level of tax complexity expands, some business owners/partners might find tax obligations difficult to adhere to. When necessary, consider finding an experienced professional to avoid noncompliance penalties.

# ◁))) Attention

The business is not required to pay tax, *"passes through"*, only partners do.

## Advantages of a Partnership

There are a vast number of benefits to starting a business partnership. In collective form, the following are advantages of participating in the partnership agreement:

- **Complementary skills:** Operating a sole proprietorship business does not give you a chance to tap skills from other people. To overcome this barrier, entering into a contractual partnership might be one of the favorable options to share valuable knowledge with others.

- **Easy and economical to form:** Compared to establishing a corporation, forming a partnership is much easier. Less paperwork is needed when being granted permission to start business operations.

- **Sharing financial obligations:** Moreover, some businesses are much riskier compared to others. As an option to minimize the risk, one might consider the so-called **"risk-sharing option"** by inviting other people into the venture.

- **Raising capital:** Reaching a sufficient level of starting capital is a challenging milestone for most prospects. In some cases, financial institutions might fail to be an immediate solution to this problem. In meeting their dreams of becoming successful business owners, most people consider starting a partnership to overcome this and other related obstacles.

- **Avoiding double tax**: In a partnership, a business does not pay double tax like corporations. Corporations are obligated to pay tax on the profit generated, the income passed on to owners and shareholders in the form of dividends or another related matter. Paying two forms of taxes is called "double tax." Double tax does not exist in partnership ventures.

## Disadvantages of a Partnership

Although the partnership is associated with numerous benefits, there are some disadvantages to participating in this type of venture. Below is a direct list of disappointing factors for being in a contract with business partners:

- **Sharing of profit:** No matter how large the profit, if your share ratio of profit is small, you will receive a reward based on your percentage of ownership. In most cases, the small portion allotted to the partners brings a disappointing atmosphere. Generally, partners who are not happy destroy the smooth continuity of the business operations.

- **Disagreement among partners:** The occurrence of any major misunderstanding might slow down daily business operations if not tackled appropriately and in a timely manner. The situation can be worse if it involves partners who play the primary role in running the business.

- **Joint liability:** Generally, most people do not like to be responsible for others' destructive responsibilities. In partnerships, you are forced to accept damages caused by other partners, whether it happened accidentally or intentionally.

# Corporations

A corporation is a more advanced form of a stand-alone (independent) business entity owned by shareholders. For tax purposes, there are two types of corporations, a *C corporation, and an S corporation.* The primary difference between the two is the way of charging corporate tax. C Corporation has *a double tax cap* while S corporation does not. The double tax cap in C corporations starts on the corporate level; the corporation is required to pay tax on the corporate net profit generated, which currently is 21 percent. Then double tax cap goes to the individual level; shareholders should pay income tax on the distributed income. On the other hand, an S corporation only pays tax on an individual level. The corporate's profit is charged tax only when it flows to the hands of shareholders.

### Additional characteristics of the corporation

- A corporation is a separate entity owned by shareholders.
- Corporations can either be for-profit or not-for-profit organizations.
- It can issue stock when preferred. Stock corporations have a charter of issuing stocks, the ownership of the corporation is determined through the stock possession.
- Non-stock Corporation is a group of entities that are not granted permission to issue stocks.

- Stock owners can be either individuals or institutions and are called stockholders.
- Compared with other forms of business entities, the corporation is one of the complex business formations with a lot of administrative fees. Moreover, the corporation has broad legal requirements to follow, including more multifaceted tax procedures compared to other entities. Because of these multidimensional procedures, the option of starting a corporation must not be taken for granted.
- The liability of stockholders does not go beyond what contributed to the business.
- The daily activities of running a corporation are left to the board of directors and not to the shareholders.
- The life of a corporation is considered perpetual. However, it can dissolve under the following circumstances; order of the court, statutory operation, and voluntary desires of the shareholders.
- Stockholders have an opportunity to transfer ownership through selling their shares in an open market or stock offerings.
- Corporations with the capability of issuing stock also have a chance of registering in a stock exchange market, called *"going public"*. It is an act of taking a private company public, which in turn, will change its ownership and be able to raise capital through selling shares. An initial public offering (IPO) is a preliminary step the corporation takes while going public.

## Forming a Corporation

When the outcomes of your research support the establishment of a corporation to forego other business entities; utilize the following procedures as primary guidance to accomplish the registration process:

- Inaugurate the business name, check for its availability, and make sure it is not hard to pronounce. The business name, along with your legal name, is required to complete the registration process

- You have a chance of filling a fictitious name in addition to the official name, if preferable. The fictitious name is also known as doing business as (DBA name), trade name, or assumed name.
- Although states laws vary; generally, at the end of the name of a corporation, it must include a corporate designation such as Corporation or Incorporated. In the United States, most corporations prefer to use Incorporated with an initial of the three letters, Inc., for example, Tropicana Inc.
- All corporations must be state-registered and will be adhered to the laws of that state.
- Register with the IRS to get an employer identification number (EIN). You will need a separate EIN for each entity you want to establish.
- Registration process takes place with your state's Secretary of State Office. It depends on the nature of the business states such as Missouri allow registering simple corporations online.
- Generally, in the registration process you will be required things such as:

  - To file articles of incorporation.
  - To pay filing fees, which vary from state to state.
  - To complete the registration report of directors.

# 🔊Attention

Some states, such as Missouri, require the corporate owners to file quarterly, biennial, or annual registration reports. Check this with your home state for more details.

## Example of a few states with the annual report requirement

| State | Report name | Submission Frequency | Due Date |
|---|---|---|---|
| Kentucky | Annual Report | Yearly | June 30 |
| Louisiana | Annual Report | Yearly | Anniversary date |
| Maine | Annual Report | Yearly | June 1 |
| Maryland | Annual Report | Yearly | April 15 |
| Massachusetts | Annual Report | Yearly | Within 2.5 months of the close of the fiscal year. |
| Michigan | Annual Report | Yearly | May 15 |
| Minnesota | Annual Renewal | Yearly | December 31 |
| Mississippi | Annual Report | Yearly | April 15 |
| Missouri | Annual Report | Yearly | Last day of the anniversary month. |

# Corporation Taxes

Tax obligations are important and mandatory that require close attention to avoid unnecessary noncompliance penalties. Below are key areas to consider:

- For-profit corporations are mandated to pay federal and state taxes. In some states, local governments also charge taxes to the corporations doing business in their territory. Do broad research to identify all additional taxes existing in your area such as sales tax.
- In case you want to change your corporation (often called C corporations) to an S corporation, to avoid double tax, you need to fill out Form 2553.
- C Corporation pays tax on the net profit made.
- To file an income tax return with IRS, corporations use Form 1120 or 1120A.
- Shareholders also pay taxes on their dividends and wages if they are employees. Nonemployees and shareholders are required to pay tax only on the distributed dividends.
- By law, corporations pay one-half of the Social Security and Medicare taxes for their employees. However, these taxes are deductible as business expenses.

# ◁))Attention

Currently, two states (South Dakota and Wyoming) do not have a corporate income tax. In addition, the same seven states, along with Alaska, Florida, Nevada, South Dakota, Texas, Washington, and Wyoming, have no personal income tax.

**Advantages of a Corporation**

Because of the abundant benefits of incorporating your business as a corporation compared to other forms of entities, the majority of businesses have been established under this article. Let's take a look at the benefits of starting and operating a corporation:

- **Limited liability:** Shareholders are enjoying the protection of their assets existing in a corporate entity. In case of any calamity, stockholders are reliable only up to income contributed to the company through shares. Only the total market value of shares presents the contribution of money the stockholders have to the corporation.

- **Creditability:** The daily business operations of a corporation are guided by many rules and regulations. Corporations are required to operate with a high level of integrity and transparency. These and other critically related factors elevate the perception and confidence in doing business with corporations. A corporation is considered a more stable business entity compared to its peers.

- **Ability to generate capital:** The corporations' credibility help them secure income easier than sole proprietorships or partnerships. Most financial institutions such as banks feel more secure when entering into contracts with corporations than other business entities. On the other hand, corporations can quickly raise working capital by selling new shares.

- **Attractive to potential employees:** Businesses are flourishing very fast due to many factors like having talented employees. Due to business set-up, operating stability, and future prosperity, among others, most corporations find it easier to secure educated, experienced, and well-committed workers above their rivals.

## Disadvantages of a Corporation

Despite having many advantages, corporations also have some drawbacks that are worth exploring. Below are disadvantages relating to the corporation business entity:

- **Double taxing:** The action of disbursing tax on business profit while paying additional tax on dividends. Double taxing discourages many participants. However, do not be discouraged by this factor alone. Your decision to pick the right form of business to start should also incorporate other factors.

- **Additional paperwork:** Extra time and resources are needed to complete any paperwork; from the time it takes registering the business to the business operating stages. Certainly, some of the rules and regulations of operating the corporation might be cumbersome to follow. If this situation applies to your site, consider utilizing the expertise of experienced personnel.

- **Voluminous fees:** Establishing corporations requires you to fill out a lot of paperwork. Also, it involves a lot of compliance rules and regulations. This tedious process consumes a lot of money, elevates business operating expenses, and minimizes profit margins.

- **Business loss:** Like other owners of business entities such as sole proprietorship and partnership, owners or shareholders in corporations do not have the privilege of deducing business loss in their tax returns.

- **Complexity:** Procedures of starting and even running a corporation business give headaches to most business owners. A lack of resources to overcome these difficulties may result in challenging times for your business.

# S Corporation

S corporation is another branch of the corporation in addition to C Corporation. Below are the primary characteristics of S corporation:

- Owners of S corporation are allowed to transfer corporate income, losses, deductions, and any available credits to shareholders. This happens during the time of filing an income tax return.
- Shareholders pay tax based on their individual tax brackets.
- S corporations do not pay double tax since the corporation is not paying tax on the corporate profit. However, corporations are accountable at the entity level for some passive income as well as build-in gains.
- Before you file for an S corporation, you have to register your business as a regular corporation in your state.
- Then you apply through IRS for the S corporation status through filing Form 2553. For the form to be accepted, all shareholders should sign the document.

When the degree of complexity starts to rise, that is the right moment to seek professional help. All essential factors should be considered in figuring out the right type of business to start. Abolish ideas of omitting key features to avoid major complications down the road.

## Seeking Business Starting Capital

Now you have decided to become a business owner. Perhaps in a few weeks, you will start searching for a building to start your restaurant. However, let me take you one step back before you decide to become the chief executive officer (CEO) of your own business. Make sure you have sufficient capital to start a functional business. The good news is that there are numerous sources of financing for your business. In case you are planning to involve external sources such as financial institutions, you need to start preparing a well-written business plan, among other requirements. The business plan will indicate how much money you need to cover starting capital and working capital as the business starts growing. Now, let's see these sources of capital and their impacts on business operations.

**Cash**: You can start your business entirely from your savings. Common sources of savings are your bank savings, which also includes retirement contributions such as 401K, traditional IRA, Roth IRA, and Simple IRA, among others. Another alternative is getting cash from your relatives, friends, coworkers, and acquaintances. Below are the advantages of financing your business through personal income:

- **Cost of capital**: When cash or other forms of personal income become starting capital for your business, the obligation of paying monthly loan interests will not be there. It is a huge relief, especially in the beginning stage of your business operations.

- **Waiting time**: The presence of cash eliminates the waiting period that you could encounter during the process of meeting the loan requirements. The advantage of having cash on hand speeds up business operations and the productivity of your venture. There is no approval process, which is common on conventional loans. Transactions that rely on bank loans require a loan seeker to prepare and present many documents. It takes additional time to be approved. Generally, all this paperwork and working time delay project operations and add business operation expenditures.

- **Collateral**: Since you have direct access to your fund, you are not required to present assets to secure your money.

- **Better deals**: In most cases, a lot of deals like purchase discounts are offered to cash holders compared to loan holders. Any reduction of business operating expenses helps to maximize profit margins.

# ◀))) Attention

Cash originating from other sources such as relatives or friends might have some pre-existing conditions that might not be in favor of your business. Moreover, you may not get the money on time as anticipated. So be prepared to come up with other alternatives when things go wrong.

**Credit card:** A good number of prospects start businesses with a combination of capital from personal savings and credit cards. Below are the outcomes of financing your business with the inclusion of a credit card.

- **Interest rate:** Of course, you have to prepare to pay an interest rate that varies from one credit card to another. Paying credit card interests increase business operating expenses. To maximize profit margin, make sure all operating expenses are justifiable including interest expenditures.

- **Waiting time:** It is an instant source of capital. No waiting time is compulsory. What you need to know are your credit limit and APR rate. From there, you are ready to execute the first transaction.

- **Collateral:** The same applies to personal cash, no assets are needed to secure funds from credit cards.

- **Limited access:** You cannot use a credit card for all transactions. For instance, you cannot pay your employee with a credit card unless you have to draw cash from it, which carries a high rate of APR. Therefore, do your research to avoid unnecessary misunderstandings or delays in your business operations.

- **Minimum monthly payment:** Minimum monthly payments on your credit cards can be a roadblock to your cash buffer. Since all cards have a specific amount of money to pay each month, the minimum amount might be bigger enough to destabilize business operations. Once again, conduct comprehensive research before using a credit card to finance your business.

- **Security:** Stories of hackers are common and are growing at an alarming speed. Since you are not immune from these hackers, you must be very alert in choosing secured places or websites before executing your transactions. Lack of precaution might jeopardize some of the transactions and slow down your business operations.

**Conventional loans:** Conventional loans have been one of the major sources of financing for most businesses around the world. Financial institutions such as banks offer these loans to borrowers who meet preexisting requirements, which are slightly different from one bank to another. Moreover, the borrower has to pay interest to cover the cost of the loan. Most of these banks charge interest every month. Depending on your credit scores, the size of the loan, and the primary purpose of the loan, collateral in the form of an asset can be requested to secure the loan. Most banks prefer immovable assets such as land or a house to secure your loan. Below are the outcomes of financing your business with a combination of conventional loans.

- **Credit score**: Your credit score has a direct impact on your loan application in the form of:
    - Receiving a loan or being denied.
    - Receiving the loan at a lower or higher interest rate.
    - Receiving the loan with or without collateral attached.
    - Receiving the loan sooner or after a prolonged period of time.

  As a loan prospect, having a higher credit score is not an option; but a prerequisite, especially when you plan to secure a better deal.

- **Waiting time:** Generally, it takes time for the banks to release the funds. The time might even be longer when you fail to submit a clean loan application. Generally, a clean loan application is one that meets all preexisting loan conditions. To cut down the waiting time and other related hassles of correcting so many items, do your homework ahead of time. Make essential efforts to understand all prerequisites relating to your loan and how to fulfill them. You can go to the bank website or call a loan manager and ask what requirements are to be satisfied before one is granted the loan. Then prepare a checklist of all requirements and work to fulfill each one.

- **Business plan:** Unfortunately, one of the requirements for conventional loans is having a well-written business plan. Experience shows that most small and medium-sized business owners do not have formal business plans. Either because they never heard about it or because they do not understand the advantages of having a business plan for their businesses. Try not to fall into this trap; it is deadly from a business perspective.

- **Brainstorming:** Do comprehensive homework before submitting any loan application. Some banks have a lot of unnecessary restrictions compared with their peers. For example, they may charge a high cost of capital compared with their rivals. To get a good deal, you need to be curious and completely educate yourself about your surroundings.

- **Interest rate:** The interest rate is also known as the annual percentage rate (APR) or cost of capital. It is one of the sensitive and well-hidden areas of the loan process. Consider the following points regarding interest rates
  - **Good deal**: Banks charge an excessive amount of interest to make a profit. Remember, you can get a good deal by considering online options or credit union banks.
  - **Payment frequency:** You need to understand and agree with the way interest is calculated, whether quarterly, semiannually, or annually.

- **Terms of the contract:** As I mentioned before, some banks have a large number of loan-related restrictions. Some of them might be harder for you to understand. Do not hesitate to ask for clarification or find legal help. Accepting the terms of the loan that you are not familiar with might put your business into trouble, or you may lose your collateral, such as a house.

- **Counseling service:** Many places offer free-of-charge business counseling services, mostly for small business owners. Make a call to your local Chamber of Commerce representative for more clarification. Most Chambers of Commerce do have in-house personnel to help the business community. Alternatively, they will direct you where you can get the help you need.

**Venture capital (VC):** This is a new form of funding for small, early-stage, or emerging businesses that have shown a promising growth rate. A venture capital firm funds your business in exchange for equity of ownership. Characteristics of venture capital are shown below:

- Venture capital is most attractive to new companies with barely noticeable operating history.
- It is offered to companies that are too small to qualify for conventional loans in the open market.
- It involves business with little or no collateral at all.

Below is a list of various groups of venture capital entities that you may consider applying for both starting and working capitals:

- **Angel investor**: Also known as *a seed investor, private investor, angel funder, business angel,* or *informal investor.* It comprises a group of wealthy investors who are willing to inject their money into start-up businesses. In return, they want to be compensated for business ownership equity or convertible debt. Characteristics of angel investors:
  - It includes a group of small but wealthy business motivated investors.
  - Ange investors can be organized online through so-called *equity crowdfunding.*
  - Also, they can organize so-called *angel networks* or *angel groups.*
  - The network group performs many duties including offering potential business advice as well as doing business research.

- **Equity crowdfunding:** Also known as *crowd investing, investment crowd investing,* or *crowd equity,* this is another online source of business start-up capital. It involves a group of investors who are term-up to raise funds to invest in commercial enterprises. The primary purpose of these investors is to receive ownership of the particular business. The greater your business is performing, the higher the stakes are. The opposite is true; when the general performance of your business is not flourishing, equity crowdfunding investors will have nothing to do except see their shares decline.

- **Seed money:** In the business world, seed money is also known as *seed capital* or *seed funding*. Here it can be a single investment injecting money into the business in exchange for an equity stake in the business. These kinds of investors are referred to as seeds because they start investing in the business while it is in its early stage until it starts generating enough cash.

The existence of several options of funds works in favor of your business. Do not be intimidated by the size and the nature of your business someone might be willing to help you once you seek help. Below are points necessary to take into consideration while preparing to pursue an external source of starting or working capital for your business:

- **Capitalize on seeking territory**: There are various sources of capital for you to miss. Just utilize all available means, including online services.

- **Maximize the level of preparation**: Before initiating any loan application, make sure you peruse the requirements since almost all are available on the company websites. See if you meet all the loan prerequisites. Even if you missed some, do not hesitate to call a bank manager for further advice. Some banks are lenient and willing to negotiate the terms of the loan contract.

- **You are a controller**: No matter how good the terms of the contract are or how persuasive the loan office is, do not sign a contract until you are confident with all terms of the contract.

- **Know your loan limit**: With the help of the business plan, you should not borrow more than what you need. Just because you qualify beyond the amount you need for your business operations does not mean you should accept more funds. Do not please the loan manager by asking to borrow more money. Remember, nothing is coming to your site for free. Down the road, the loan interest may be too much for you to handle. In return, it might jeopardize the future operations of your business.

- **Evaluate the payback period**: Make sure that you can afford the monthly payment that includes principal and interest. Also, evaluate how long it takes to pay back the full loan amount. Once again, your business plan will facilitate you in reaching the right answers.

- **Business plan**: Prepare a comprehensive business plan – stronger enough to persuade a loan officer from the very beginning. You have to elaborate on the exact purpose of your business and how you plan to make money or generate enough profit from your idea. In other words, you need to tell them in a few sentences how marketable your idea is versus your rivals.

## What you need to take to the lender

Each lender has different documentation requirements compared to another. Research what is needed by contacting your bank loan manager. Below are common requirements for most lenders:

# Common Requirements

| Factor | New Business | Existing Business |
|---|---|---|
| Purpose of the loan | Yes | Yes |
| History of the business | No | Yes |
| Last three years' financial statements | No | Yes |
| Projected three years of financial statements | Yes | Yes |
| Broad details and schedule of term debts | No | Yes |
| Aging of accounts receivable and payable | No | Yes |
| Lease agreement details | Yes | Yes |
| Amount of investment in the business by the owner(s) | Yes | Yes |
| Signed personal financial statements | No | Yes |
| Personal resume(s) | Yes | Yes |
| List of reference | Yes | Yes |

# The Six Cs

In addition to the aforementioned common requirements lenders need to see, the loan evaluation process also goes deeper into small but important aspects that the lenders deemed necessary to ignore. They include what are so-called "the six Cs" that comprise:

- Characters of the loan applicant(s).
- Capacity to pay the loan back.
- The capital needed.
- Collateral to secure the loan.
- General conditions of the loan.
- The degree of confidence of the borrowers.

The broad details of the six Cs are revealed below:

## The Six Cs

| Factor | Description |
|---|---|
| Character | Lenders also pay attention to your moral obligation and total commitments on loan repayments. They use the credit and payment history as a starting factor, followed by looking at the pledges mentioned on your business plan. |
| Capacity to pay | Lenders want to minimize the risk as much as they can by conducting a comprehensive analysis of your (borrower) past, present, and projected financial statements. Moreover, the evaluation includes other |

important information, such as the other features of your business plan.

**Capital**  Financiers are not there just to pour money on you. They want to evaluate your financial stability and how your business will maximize ROI, among others. They measure financial stability and make sure you have low debt-to-asset and debt-to-worth ratios. Moreover, lenders want your business to have high current ratios.

**Collateral**  A collateral is a lender's asset(s) pledged against the loan in case of failure to pay. Most lenders prefer the value of collateral to be closer to the amount of the loan offered. They prefer immovable items such as houses, farms, and land, among other things. Alternatively, you may find someone to cosign your loan.

**Conditions**  The prevailing conditions, such as geopolitical, general economic, geographic, and industry trends, are given significant weight.

**Confidence**  Creditors eventually grade the factors listed above (the five Cs) to come up with a measure of the borrower's confidence level. The higher the rate, the better the chance to secure the full loan amount you have requested.

# Loan Appraisal Tipoffs

When you decide to finance your business whole or partially with debts, your business will be on the defensive side against leaders. The loan manager will primarily concentrate on your ability to repay the loan. The determination of creditworthiness will be determined by looking at your business credit report and possibly; personal credit report, as well. Before submitting any loan applications, check with all credit bureaus (consumer reporting agencies) to verify the accuracy of your business records. The same applies to all signatory executives whose names and signatures will appear on the loan forms. Below is the list of the primary consumer reporting agencies:

### Consumer Reporting Agency

**Agency**          **Contact Information**


**Equifax**

> Web site: www.equifax.com
> Mailing address:
> > Equifax Credit Information
> > Services, Inc.
> > P.O. Box 740241
> > Atlanta, GA 30374
> Phone number:
> > 1-888-202-4025

## Experian

Web site: www.experian.com
Mailing address:
    Experian
    475 Anton Blvd
    Costa Mesa, CA 92626
Phone number:
    714 830 7000
**or**
    Experian
    955 American Lane
    Schaumburg, IL 60173
Phone number:
    222 698 5600

## TransUnion

Web site: www.transunion.com
Mailing address:
    Annual Credit Report Request
    Service

    P.O. Box 105281

    Atlanta, GA 30348-5281

Phone:
    877-322-8228 (Personal)
    844-245-4071 (Business)

# ◁))) Attention

## Tips for Borrowing

- In most cases, financial institutions do not finance the entire business. So prepare to come up with at least one-third of the starting capital.
- Before your first appointment, make sure you prepare all the necessary documents to secure your loan ahead of time. You may decide to call a loan officer for more clarification.
- First impressions matter. So make sure you dress neat and professionally on your appointment day.
- Before seeking funds from financial institutions, research first government-funded grants and loans. Small business administration (SBA) is one of the government institutions created to help small and medium-sized enterprises. I highly encourage you to visit its website. It has a lot of useful information for prospects. Here is the link: https://www.sba.gov
- Make sure your business is well prepared to maximize the chance of getting the loan you need. You may consider involving professionals if you are venerable in some areas of preparing a comprehensive business plan.
- In case you are not sure, consult your accountant to discuss what type of loan you need and the necessary steps to follow.
- To maximize in your favor the outcomes of the interview, you have to develop a habit of being a good listener.

No matter the size of the loan you want to get from lenders, having sufficient preparations ahead of time is a key technique to maximize the chance of securing a good deal. Show the lender your degree of maturity in business rather than being there to waste their time. Maintain a high level of professionalism accompanied by a comprehensive business plan. Importantly, you want to give the lenders a piece of mind knowing that their money will be in good hands. Moreover, assure them that there is a high chance of getting their money back in full plus the indicated ROI. Either way, you should make strong preparations, going through all options of raising enough capital, including looking at the pros and cons of each option.

## Business registration

After having an assurance of getting enough working capital to start your restaurant business, register your business. Only the federal tax rate is flat regardless of where you live in the United States. However, that is not the case when it comes to the city and the state taxes. Some cities or states are charging higher taxes, and some are not. They differ in the level of incentives to support business owners, especially the new ones. Consider calling the Chamber of Commerce in your local area to explore existing incentives in the restaurant industry without forgetting about the new business owners. Below are procedures for registering your business:

- **Register your business name:** Start by calling or going online to see if the name is available versus those that are already taken. Remember, no state allows one name to be used with more than one business. Below is an example of how to search businesses in these states:

    In the state of Missouri:

    1. Website: https://www.sos.mo.gov/
    2. Phone: (573) 751-4153.
    3. Email: corporations@sos.mo.gov.

In the state of Nevada:
1. Website: http://nvsos.gov/sos.
2. Phone: 775-684-5708.
3. Email: sosmail@sos.nv.gov.

In Washington state:
1. Visit the Business Name Database. Visit the Washington Office of the Secretary of State website.
2. Search your Business Name. Enter the name you would like to use in the "Corporation Search" section of the site. ...
3. Review Results

- **Register with state and local agencies**: Most states and local governments have an online protocol system of saving their customers conveniently in addition to calling or visiting the local offices. Use whichever means works better for you. If you are filing for a corporation, you will also need to file articles of incorporation, whereby an LLC needs to file an article of organization. Remember, slight procedural differences might exist from one state to another; the same applies to the local governments.

Since you are planning to hire employees in your business, do not forget to apply for the state tax ID number that needs to be shown on each of your employees' W2 forms. Since the procedures for hiring employees differ from one state to another; contact your state department of labor for more details. Generally, it is cheap and easy to work with independent contractors compared with dealing with employees concerning the city and state procedures compliance.

**Register with the IRS:** You can apply for an employer identification number (EIN) with the IRS online, by fax, or by mail.

Complete all areas in Form SS-4 and make sure you sign it before submitting it to the IRS. Your form will be denied if it is missing essential information, including the signature of the applicants. In addition, make sure you know the business structure you want to pursue and a tax year that works better for your venture. For online fillers, use this link: https://www.irs.gov/businesses/small-businesses-self-employed.

In case you plan to hire employees in your business, you have to indicate that followed by filling out additional forms, such as Form I-9 and Form W-4. Use Form I-9 to verify the identity and employment authorization of individuals hired for employment in the United States. All U.S. employers must properly complete Form I-9 for each individual they hire for employment in the United States. Form W-4 tells you, as the employer, the employee's filing status, multiple jobs adjustments, amount of credits, and amount of other income, amount of deductions, etc.

In some other types of businesses, their owners have a moral duty of applying for licenses and permits as the final step of business registration. However, in the restaurant business, you can apply for a permit when the needs arise during the process of repairing the building. The task of looking for the repair permits is get done by contractors and not by the business owner. For the food-related permits, it is your duty as a business owner to seek them.

# Additional factors needed to run a successful business

While you are in the process of starting your business, make sure you consider other small but essential elements of running a functional and effective business, such as:

**Business name:** Come up with an easy and memorable name for your customers. Before you start printing business cards or purchasing a domain name, check if it's available in your home state. Remember, a lot of states allow you to complete the process online.

**Business logo:** Design an attractive and business-inclusive emblem that represents the identity of your venture in all printouts and online. It has to be unique so it can withstand the competition of other existing logos in the arena. The logo should be simple and exude excellence.

**Build a website:** A detailed website presents your ideas inclusively and inexpensively. Make sure you build a website that contains all essential links based on your business model. If possible, try to avoid HTML and go ahead with a database website that allows you as an administrator to edit contents, pictures, or video clips any time at your convenience. You might be charged slightly more for electing a database website, but the advantages of this choice are worth undertaking in the long run compared with the hassle of calling the developer anytime you need to edit the content on your website.

Shop around! There is a lot of competition among website builders, which forces some of them to accept a small fee. They want to have something to do rather than go days without having any tangible project at their disposal. Make sure you agree with the developer about the option of performing many reviews with no additional fees until you get a well-functional website with the same original price.

**Print business cards:** Business cards speak much about your business and your level of seriousness as a business owner. So try to develop attractive but also inclusive business cards that communicate the message of your business well. A website like Vista Print (https://www.vistaprint.com), has a plethora of templates to choose from for almost any business. It allows you to develop the card from scratch and upload pictures or logos to your template. These fixtures allow you to develop attractive cards that fit your business model. They are also much cheaper compared to most printing companies in the market. The rule of thumb is to make sure you do a lot of research before agreeing with a developer. Indeed, appealing cards present a valuable image of your business. It is a killer spear you should always strive to have with you.

**Purchase a business phone:** This business needs a phone that is reliable and capable of performing a lot of functions, also high-speed internet. Choose a provider with good coverage and strong signals. Some of the benefits of having a reliable and well functional mobile phone are:
- It facilitates improving customer service.
- It allows you to have constant contact with the office, customers, and suppliers from anywhere.
- The phone plays a major role to increase productivity.
- When necessary, it facilitates working remotely.

**Purchase well-designed furniture:** Make sure you have all the essential features that support the functionality of a good office and your employees. Constantly aim to maintain a high level of professionalism. Try to purchase a cheap but nice desk and comfortable executive office chair. Also, do not forget to have a bookshelf with locked drawers for keeping valuable items. Moreover, the furniture for the break room must be durable to withstand the high frequency of employees who are taking breaks regularly.

# Open a bank account

Having a business account separate from your account is very important and highly recommended. Do this immediately before you start operating your business. From a legal and tax perspective, all business transactions should be separate and clear from expenditures or income that directly benefits the manager without excluding the owner. The procedure of opening a business account takes a few minutes or hours, depending on the bank you are doing business with and the documents needed. Banks do not maintain uniform standards of opening business accounts. Any differences should be addressed by phone before visiting your preferred bank. Alternatively, you can conduct detailed research on the bank's website. Due to the existence of Covid-19, some banks do not allow walk-ins, so make an appointment ahead of time to avoid unnecessary disturbances.

Below is a list of common documents that most banks constantly ask their customers to bring before start opening an account:
- Personal identification
- Employer identification number (EIN) or social security number (SSN)
- Business license
- Article of incorporation: It depends on the form of the business you want to start
- Business address
- Partnership agreement if applicable
- Charter and Bylaws of Association or copy of minutes of the last meeting with newly elected officers, if applicable in your business.

Try to validate the information you are getting online by calling the bank directly. Since the occurrence of the Covid-19, it makes banks implement many changes without warming. These rapid changes often got forgotten to be inserted into the website in a timely manner. Moreover, some new changes might be applicable in some branches and not centralized by the head office, which controls all online information.

# Locating a restaurant building

Location location location x 10!

This is a song all business owners are advised to memorize and sing day and night while looking for a place to rent for their restaurant businesses. Do not sign any contract just because the rent is unbeatable. When it is time to pick a building for your restaurant, there are many important factors to consider in addition to monthly rent. Some of the decisive factors are mentioned next page:

- **Size of the building:** Make sure you understand your needs before you start looking at the building. Prepare the number and size of tables you need and where the counter will be located. If you plan to have a waiting area include that in your layout. If you plan to offer buffet service, do not omit its location. Next, measure the distance between each table before coming up with the total square footage for the dining room. To get the size of the building, add the square footage of the dining area with the kitchen, bathroom, storage, breakroom, and office areas. Depending on your needs, you can eliminate a room such as an office. Instead of an office, you can add something else that you think is important to meet the needs of your layout.

- **Accessibility:** Make sure the building is easily accessible, even for employees and customers. Also, pay attention to the condition of the road. It should be in good condition. Avoid establishing your business in a flooded area. You do not want your business to experience isolation due to floods.

- **Rent:** With no discussion, make sure the rent is justifiable based on the size, structure, location, and age of the building. If possible, ask your neighbor how long they have been renting and how much the rent was initially. You also need to know how frequently the rent will increase and the amount. This is a section of the contract where fine print plays a big role. You might be celebrating paying a small about of rent right now without knowing the landlord is just persuading you to sign the contract. Then after one year, it is when the time for you to pay the price will start. You might see the rent increase beyond your control. Make sure you ask all basic questions before entering into a legal contract.

- **Hidden costs:** Ask the landlord to reveal to you all costs associated with the building, including the cost of rush, snow removal, and lawn care. Remember, an important point most new customers miss is the cost of repairing or replacing a water heater, air conditioning unit, and heater. If you are responsible for these units, make sure the current ones are almost new; and they receive all the essential services they need. Try to ask for the receipts to justify the landlord's claims.

- **Security:** Try to locate a place with a low crime rate. A place where you feel comfortable installing equipment without worrying that someone will steal or vandalize them overnight. Also, you have to consider the security of your customers. When necessary, install enough lights and cameras to ensure the environment is secure.

- **Speed limit:** Avoid renting a building in a place where the speed limit is above 45 miles an hour. When the speed limit increases, it's harder for new customers to see your building or decide to stop; unless you have enough customer base. Otherwise, there will not be an influx of new customers if you ignore this crucial decisive factor. It should not be taken for granted.

- **Parking lot:** Make sure the size of the parking lot meets the maximum number of customers you are expecting to serve daily or per designated time slots.

- **Fitting with the brand image:** Before you sign the contract, you have to pay attention to the structure and the look of the building to make sure it complements your brand's image. For example, if you are planning to sell Mexican food and you signed a contract for a building with an Italian structure, you will sabotage your business before it opens. In this scenario, you might change the image of the building before you start the business. The question is, who will cover the repair expenses? This and other related issues should be analyzed in detail before signing the contract.

- **Legal considerations:** Make sure the contract has all information that you have discussed or agreed to with the landlord. Also, it must explain how the legal process will be managed and in which jurisdiction.

- **Room to grow (if necessary):** If you are expecting to expand your business in the same building, then come up with a plan ahead of time to avoid unnecessary hiccups down the road.

- **Competition in the area:** Pay close attention to the competitors who are selling the same type of food. Importantly, it is useless to enter into battle with your rivals that you cannot win whatsoever.

- **The age of the building:** Older buildings are so expensive to take care and they have constant problems that are hard to predict. When you think this is the only option to go, try to set aside a sizeable budget for repaid expenses.

- **Nature of contract:** Ask a landlord to give you enough time to read the entire contract before signing. If necessary, read it more than once to maximize the level of understanding. With the help of relatives or friends, when necessary, you decide if the terms are within your ability to handle them or not. However, when a tough situation arises, and it seems that more negotiations are needed, you may consider involving your lawyer. Moreover, you may decide to walk away from the situation if you and the landlord can't come to any terms of the agreement.

- **Duration of contract:** Before you sign the lease agreement, it is a good idea to figure out the length of your contract. Assume a landlord is asking you to sign a five or seven-year contract while you are new in this business. What will happen if your business model is not working to the point you have to close operations to save some money? Who wants to be stuck with a building that they're not using? You may start with a lease that lasts three years. This is a standard contract most new business owners prefer to sign. When you start experiencing positive results in your business, you can sign a long-duration agreement. At this point, your business vision should be functional and profitable.

Choosing a location to start your business is a challenging decision that's not worth taking for granted. It involves many decisive factors that require close attention. The list is not exhaustive, which makes it easier to include additional factors that suit your business model. Anytime you think the process is heading in the wrong direction, consider seeking professional help. The goal is to maximize the chance of getting a good deal beneficial for your business in the long run.

**Summary**

The efforts to explore important information for starting your business are worth undertaking. You need to be familiar with all procedures of starting a functional and productive business from day one. Going this route will help you solve a lot of challenges other new business owners are facing while transitioning into this new journey. The fewer obstacles you face, the higher the chances are for your business to have a solid start, which is a great relief. In the end, a state-of-the-art preparation plan with you maximizes the chances of generating a huge ROI.

# To-Do List Form – Chapter Three

| Action | Goals | Results(Y/N) |
|---|---|---|
| **Time-sensitive actions:**<br><br>1.<br><br>2.<br><br>3.<br><br>4.<br><br>5.<br><br>6.<br><br>7.<br><br>8.<br><br>9.<br><br>10. | | |
| **Less time-sensitive actions**<br><br>1.<br><br>2.<br><br>3.<br><br>4. | | |

| | | |
|---|---|---|
| 5. | | |
| 6. | | |
| 7. | | |
| 8. | | |
| 9. | | |
| 10. | | |

# Read Again Pages – Chapter Three

| Page # | Topic/Subtopic | Purpose | Result (Y/N) |
|---|---|---|---|
| | | | |
| | | | |
| | | | |
| | | | |
| | | | |

# Chapter Four

## Setting a comprehensive operational structure

Now that you have built the foundation of your business, it is time to look at the essential steps of forming a sound operational structure. One that is required to run a profitable business. You must prepare a detailed plan for executing all essential tasks before the grand opening date. The plan should identify each task and how to accomplish it. The execution plan should include the time frame needed to finish each task. The individuals who will perform each task also must be included. Address the standards or expectations of the outputs ahead of time. Be realistic by preparing a plan B for each task in case of the failure of the original plans.

# Type of restaurant you can start

The availability of various choices to pick from before deciding which type of restaurant to start offers you the basic flexibility any newcomer gets. Utilize these options to your benefit before coming up with a better business model that fits the needs of your target customers; meanwhile, it must fall within your primary vision. Since we have seen the importance of specializing in one area or field, explore types of restaurants before choosing one that complements your future.

- **Fast food restaurant:** This type of restaurant deals with the sale of food that has already been pre-prepared. Alternatively, it deals with food that takes a shorter time to arrange. Their customers want to find a quick dish that is ready to eat inside the restaurant or takeout. Examples of these restaurants are McDonald's, KFC, Burger King, and others.

- **Fast-casual dining:** It includes restaurants that cook food from scratch. The majority of their customers prefer to eat inside the restaurants. It includes café, pub, and family-style dining, to name a few.

- **Upscale restaurant:** The list comprises restaurants that possess the following characteristics:
  - They sell expensive food and beverages.
  - They offer high-quality dishes.

  They target customers of a high social class. Here are some examples of restaurants that fit in this category: The Melting Pot, Morton's Steakhouse, Palm Restaurant, and Fleming's Prime Steakhouse, among others.
- **Food truck:** In this case, your restaurant will be located in a motorized vehicle or trailer rather than a brick and mortar. You can preserve a variety of foods, such as frozen food, pre-packaged food made from scratch, or food prepared in a commercial kitchen.

- **Pop up a restaurant without a long-term commitment:** It is another way of executing your dreams. However, the discussion of this book does not include this group of business owners.

Based on the definition of each class, there is a solid line that differentiates each category from the other. You will have a wide selection to pick the right type of restaurant for launch. However, do not take this opportunity for granted. You have to brush up on your business models and ensure you select the right option. You need to have a restaurant where you enjoy working and be willing to sacrifice every minute of your life to maximize every step of operating milestones.

## Setting the dining room

It is the right time to put your interior design talent into practice. Arranging the restaurant dining room is the same as setting up your sitting room. However, in this case, you have to add your design skills on a big scale. Even though you might have a little bit of a problem in the designing area, help is at your fingertips. There are a lot of interior designers specializing in this industry. Consider seeking their help when you encounter challenges while arranging your business dining room.

Rather than treating the task of designing a dining room as a whole set, the process can be divided to simplify the task. You can come up with any simple ways of forming subprojects as shown below:

- **Sitting capacity:** This is an important section that helps in the planning process of many things. Generally, the city personnel will provide you with the maximum capacity for customers. The number is based on the size of your dining room. Other small

decisive factors include seating arrangements, location, the size of the counter, availability of the waiting area, and others.
- **Dining table:** Come up with the right size for the dining table. Moreover, the texture of the materials used to make the table also matters. Chose the right height to suit the needs of your target customers.

- **Table lamp:** If small table lamps work for you, place them on each table. Try to identify the right color of the lamps and the attractive design. Avoid cheap items that do not have any appealing power or have lower safety ratings.

- **Color:** When utilized properly, a combination of various colors can make the dining room of your restaurant look beautiful and inviting. If you are not good at choosing the right colors, you may hire a professional to help you.

- **Ceiling lights:** Having ceiling lights or chandeliers is a game-changer when you know how to pick the right brand. Also, the light fixtures should complement the color of the floor, ceiling, and all sidewalls.

- **Floor:** Remember, a home setting is not the same as a business look. For each type of floor, you will select whether tiles, carpet, hardwood, or a combination of either one will be a part of your design plan. If you plan to have a combination of tiles and woods, make sure you choose the appropriate ratio and the right locations for installment.

Here are some things to pay attention to when deciding on the decor of your restaurant:
- The type of materials
- The color of the walls
- How the final look will complement other items in the room

# Additional things to consider

As you continue to arrange the dining room of your restaurant, pay attention to other essential factors such as:

- **Wall fixtures:** All items placed on the wall should have a purposeful reason to be there and should complement your business model and the look of the other items, such as materials and color of the floor, walls, light fixtures, counter, ceiling, and others.

- **Type of wine:** No matter how delicious your food is; in case you will be selling wines in your restaurant, try to have the most popular brands to meet the desires of your customers. Customers who belong in this category are never pleased with only food; they want to enjoy the meals with their favorite signature wines.

- **Table linens:** For those who want to use table linens to decorate tables, make sure you pick nice materials with attractive colors to complement the entire look of the dining room.

- **Meals:** Unless your restaurant is serving fast food, avoid telling the customer to look over the wall to see what they want to eat. All menus must be printed on nice, hard paper with attractive pictures of the most popular meals you serve.

- **Toilet:** All considerations of arranging the dining room discussed above should be put into consideration while remodeling the toilet. Remember, this is a very important section of your business.

- **The dining room.** Avoid cutting corners during the time of remodeling or building the toilet. Have a functional cleaning plan in place. Customers tend to have a perception of the look of the toilet and compare it with other inaccessible rooms such as the kitchen or storage room. If they find the toilet is constantly dirty, they will start thinking the food they eat is unsanitary. Therefore, expect to see your customers going to your competitors to get the better service you failed to offer them.

- **Cashier desk:** It is another item appearing in the dining room. Consider many factors before you build it including:
  - size of the desk
  - the location
  - the height of the desk
  - materials needed to build the desk
  - easy accessibility
  - if security is an issue in your area, figure out how it will be handled
  - location and the number of drawers
  - location and the type of the security button, if applicable

The list is not exhaustive. Go through your business model and come up with supplementary things that need to be implemented before the opening day of your dream restaurant.

## How the utensils and other stuff should be arranged

After knowing which types of tables will be in your restaurant, it is important to understand how the utensils should be arranged on the table. Below is the list of the basic utensils that you can find in most restaurants and the recommended setting:

- **Forks:** Go to the left-hand side.
- **Oyster fork**: It goes to the right-hand side with the knives.
- **Knives:** Put them on the right-hand side.
- **Glassware:** Is placed above the knives.
- **Dessert spoon:** It goes above the plate.

- **Napkins:** Should be placed either underneath the forks or to the left of the forks.
- **A charger plate:** Should be placed in the center.
- **Serving plate:** Should be placed in the middle with the charger plate.
- **A glass of water or coffee:** Generally, it is optional, but in most cases, they go slightly to the right-hand side.

Unfortunately, most customers especially the middle and premier class understand the order of these things. When you want to target these groups of customers, make sure you do your homework ahead of time rather than waiting for bad reviews to start appearing on your business social media page. In the business world, it is a little bit expensive to correct bad reviews compared with taking constructive actions ahead of time. Constantly, strive to beat customer expectations and go beyond.

## Setting a kitchen

Productivity in your restaurant will start in the kitchen before it starts flowing into other areas. Do not expect to set a larger space for the kitchen just because the landlord allows you to build dry walls that suit your needs. When you go down that route, the remaining space might not be enough to accommodate other things, such as the dining room, toilet, counter, bar center if you need one, and more. To avoid this nightmare, the concept of designing your kitchen should be taken seriously.

The key point is for you to have a normal size kitchen, but with an ability to look big after being well organized. For this concept to happen, the kitchen should be thoroughly set up for all essential activities to take place without any sign of hiccups. These basic kitchen activities have been divided into five categories mentioned below:

- washing station
- food preparation area
- cooking station
- service area
- storage area

Each section must be well located and set up to allow activities to flow in a soundly synchronized manner. To make sure this process is happening, arrange the kitchen in either of the following categories:

1. **Assembly line:** Under this layout, the arrangement starts with food preparation first, followed by meal cooking, service areas, dishwashing station, and finally, the storage room. The planning of each category is in the form of the line as it appears in the blueprint below: food preparation, then cooking dishes, and finally, saving the meals to the customers. Chipotle is a good example of a kitchen layout of this nature.

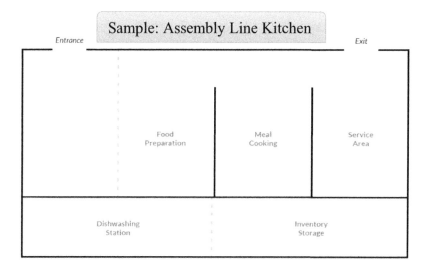

Sample: Assembly Line Kitchen

| | | |
|---|---|---|
| Entrance | | Exit |

Food Preparation

Meal Cooking

Service Area

Dishwashing Station

Inventory Storage

2. **Island layout:** With the exception of having a cooking place in the middle of the kitchen, all other stations are allocated around the kitchen. Latour restaurant used this style in their kitchen.

Sample: Island Layout Kitchen

Entrance                                    Exit

Dishwashing Station

Service Area

Meal Cooking

Inventory Storage

Food Preparation

3. **Zone-style layout**: The layout of the kitchen should be sectioned on a zonal basis, as shown below. Big commercial kitchens and catering kitchens are good examples of the primary users of this style.

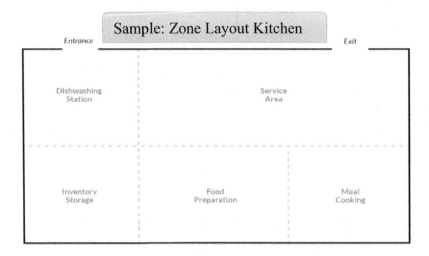

Sample: Zone Layout Kitchen

4. **Galley layout:** This option works well for the long narrow space. Whereby, all stations are allocated on one side of the room. All food trucks are organizing their kitchens this way.

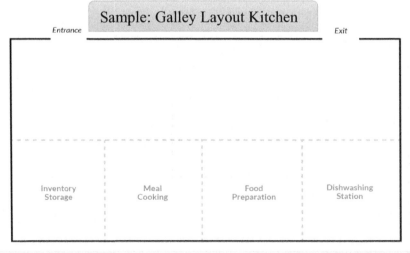

Sample: Galley Layout Kitchen

5.  **Open kitchen layout:** Few restaurants prefer to choose this type of setting, such as Panda Express. They want to assure their customer that they are getting fresh and clean food as much as possible. If you want to try this option, make sure all hot cooking areas and pans are far away from the reach of the customers.

The choice of the kitchen plan starts with your business model and the type of restaurant you want to start. Since it costs a sizeable amount of money to build a kitchen of any style, try to explore all options ahead of time before making the final decision. The decision to demolish the previous kitchen to build the new one can be done with no doubt. But it will cost you a substantial amount of money. The cost and time to accomplish the tasks are a big deal, especially when the budget is tight. Selecting the right style from the very beginning is one of the preferable options to save your money and time.

## How to maximize the exterior look of the building

The first impression of your restaurant starts with the outside of the building. Customers in the food industry have a lot of alternatives to choose from. Unless you take bold action to elevate your identity, all other efforts of investing in this business might be destroyed with no reward to compensate you. Pay attention to these key external issues before you open your business:

*   **Canopy and window:** They should always be kept clean, before and after the business resumes its operations.

*   **Lawn and plants:** Try to water your lawn to look green all the time. Cut your lawn as recommended to maximize its beauty. Plants, including flowers and trees, should be evenly trimmed. Be sure they are of the right height and shape as well. Also, replace missing plants immediately.

- **Smoking area:** If you have a designated smoking place outside your restaurant, take great care of it. It is easy to be forgotten, especially when the owner is a nonsmoker.

- **Parking lot:** It should be clean with no potholes. Install enough lights to maximize security and give peace of mind to customers. Moreover, replace the burnout bulbs much sooner.

- **Cleanness:** The surrounding areas of your business should be very clean. If you cannot do it yourself, assign one of your employees to inspect the exterior of the building daily. You may consider increasing the number of inspections to be more than once daily; it depends on the general behavior of your customers.

- **Patio:** A lot of restaurants serve meals on the patio. If you want to apply the same idea, start by exploring all the essential things for this plan to happen, such as the location and the size of the patio. Also, the zone of the area where your restaurant is located is another decisive factor. The point here is you must make sure the patio area is not forgotten. It is part of your restaurant and customers understand that, so do you.

The general outlook of your business has a direct impact on the minds of your new and existing customers and whether or not they decide to keep coming to your restaurant. When you believe that your design ideas are running short, do not hesitate to seek help from professionals. There are a lot of designers in each corner of our cities. However, they differ in the quality of their outputs and the fees they charge per project. When necessary, request more than three quotes before deciding on the right person to help you. More than ever, this is the right moment to share this concept with your winning club members. First to get their opinions and secondly, to help you with referral ideas if they know someone who is good in the designing field.

# To-Do List Form – Chapter Four

| Action | Goals | Results(Y/N) |
|---|---|---|
| **Time-sensitive actions:**<br><br>1.<br><br>2.<br><br>3.<br><br>4.<br><br>5.<br><br>6.<br><br>7.<br><br>8.<br><br>9.<br><br>10. | | |
| **Less time-sensitive actions**<br><br>1.<br><br>2.<br><br>3.<br><br>4. | | |

| | | |
|---|---|---|
| 5. | | |
| 6. | | |
| 7. | | |
| 8. | | |
| 9. | | |
| 10. | | |

# Read Again Pages – Chapter Four

| Page # | Topic/Subtopic | Purpose | Result (Y/N) |
|---|---|---|---|
|  |  |  |  |
|  |  |  |  |
|  |  |  |  |
|  |  |  |  |
|  |  |  |  |

# Chapter Five

## Procedures for building a functional team

When the time comes to build a team of employees, you need to inspect what is needed for your restaurant to operate smoothly. Discuss all factors that have the potential to impact service. Your business model and plan should possess enough insight into the number of shifts needed, the number of employees designated for each shift, and opening and closing hours.

### The shift in the restaurant industry

Depending on your business model, you can choose any type of shift that works better for your business. Alternatively, consider implementing a combination of shifts to suit your desires. However, avoid coming up with complicated shifts that will be hard for your employees to adopt. Listed below are a few shift ideas you may want to consider:

- **Fixed shift:** Under this shift, employees will be working the same shift each week. It is one of the easiest shifts to schedule with a lot of work stability. Employees working this kind of shift enjoy the predictability of working hours. However, the shift limits the flexibility of the business owners. Constantly, it allows occurrences of understaffed or overstaffed in either shift.

- **Rotation shift:** Creating schedules like this for employees means they will rotate breakfast, lunch, or dinner shifts. Alternatively, the shift can be arranged week to week or month to month. This technique works best for restaurants that operate 24/7. Also, it allows a lot of flexibility for the owner though most employees do not like working this way.

- **Split shift:** When you choose this shift, employees will be working two different shifts within one day. Business owners love it because it helps to balance the number of staff based on the availability of customers. Be aware that the shift contributes to a lot of burnout with employees and it costs much more to pay split shifts. Moreover, some states are stricter on this type of shift. So do your homework to stay on the safe side of the law.

- **Swing shift:** It is when employees start working late afternoon to evening hours. It provides the owner with enough personnel to serve customers at high-demand times. Most employees also prefer it because they get enough time to do personal commitments in the morning before work time. However, the family-oriented workers never like this shift since it separates them from their family members in the evening hours.

- **On-call shift:** Employees on this shift show up to work when you need them. You call them when the crowd starts to increase and send them home during slow hours. It helps to avoid overstaffing and helps control payroll. In addition, more workers enjoy this form of flexibility that allows them to work when they like. However, some employees do not like this unpredictable schedule because it causes their pay to fluctuate.

- **Overtime shift:** It occurs when you allow employees to work more than 40 hours a week. It helps you to get staff when you need them. On the flip side, employees prefer to get extra hours to meet their goals of getting a big paycheck. But you have to be very careful with this method since it is one of the major contributors to inflated payroll expenditures. Additionally, pay closer attention to the Fair Labor Standards Act (FLSA). The act mandates all employers to pay one and a half for all hours worked above 40 average hours per week.

- **No schedule work schedule:** Employers adopt this shift when they want their employees to work randomly or to meet their demands. It is one of the complicated shifts that I cannot recommend to any of my customers or friends like you.

The number of shifts is broad enough for you to pick the one that works better for your restaurant. It is common to apply more than one shift when the need arises. However, when you decide to do that, make sure you take all necessary precautions to avoid confusion on your side and the employees'.

## Business open hours

The time of operating your restaurant is another important decision to plan ahead of time to avoid confusion down the road. Deeply explore the eating behavior of your customers, which will play a huge role in setting the right hours of opening for your restaurant. It is a good idea to assess the operations hours of your competitors before coming up with the right and more productive hours. Generally, most restaurants open their door at 11:00 am. However, some of them are opening earlier, between 10:00 am - 10:30 am. The general closing time is 9:00 pm. The restaurants that serve liquor; in most cases, they close later.

# Hours of work

After developing a workable shift with the help of the winning equation shown in chapter three, sit down and develop hours of work per shift, each day, week, and perhaps monthly. Remember, some or all employees who work the morning shift must arrive at least one hour early. The opposite is true too. Some employees on the last shift should stay past closing time to perform after-work activities such as cleaning, washing dishes, and more.

Remember, you do not need to ask workers of all first shifts to come early, just a few of them based on your needs. The same concept applies to the last shift. Only employees with tangible assigned duties are the ones who should stay after closing hours. The primary purpose of this decision is to minimize payroll expenses, which are a huge portion of the total operating expenditures of most businesses.

## Number of employees needed

Although it is hard to predict with certainty the number of customers you will be getting on a weekly or monthly basis, you must project a number. You need this proposed number to figure out the number of employees for each working time frame. The combination of hours of work and the number of staff you need helps prepare the payroll budget. As always, underestimating the amount of cash or cash equivalent needed in a particular period is as bad as overestimating the figure.

It might be a little complicated at the beginning of your business operations. Yet, with time, the process of computing the payroll budget will become easier for you. That being said, feel free to consult your accountant to help you figure out how to predict the number of customers and the total number of employees to hire. Also, do not forget to ask for assistance in scheduling those employees. Create a schedule that maximizes the productivity of each employee while minimizing the total operating expenses. When you prosper on this issue, the chance of maximizing ROI will increase.

# Types of staff to hire

Generally, most staff in restaurants have specialty duties to perform. Some can work in more than one position, and some just fit only one skill. To assist you with the hiring process, let us explore the basic categories of employees you need:

- **Front employees:** It comprises servers and hostesses who specialize in working with customers face to face.
- **Back employees:** The list covers the people who are preparing and cooking the food. Also, it includes dishwashers.
- **Outside employees:** Some restaurants do have people who are working to assist with directing customers where to park their cars or moving them when the queue is longer than usual.
- **Support staff:** This is a list of managerial levels. The managers are the ones dealing with planning procedures, implementing the blueprints, and being accountable for the final results.

Once you have identified the type of team you need, it facilitates the development of the functional list of employees needed and their qualifications. Although some employees are willing and capable of overlapping from one position to another, not all fall into this category. As a manager, try to be wise enough to understand the capability of your employees and the importance of having a proper balance of employees on each shift based on their degree of capabilities. The collective concept behind this task is to elevate productivity to the highest level possible.

# Quality of employees to hire

Unfortunately, working in the food industry requires a lot of good personalities to get the job done right. With the help of the winning members, try to explore all the options on the table to recruit employees willing to move with you while executing your vision. You can benefit from employees with a team-building spirit, capable and willing to go the extra mile without losing their composure. Some of the recommended traits to pay attention to at the time of recruiting are:

- **Quick learners:** Try to hire employees that can learn new things much faster.

- **Enthusiasm:** Definitely, select workers who love their job and are willing to work without complaining. The ones with a high level of keenness.

- **Working faster**: Choose those who demonstrate an ability to work faster since this is one of the fastest moving industries. Statistics show that slower employees play a major role in slowing down the productivity level of any business. Of course, your business will not be immune to this issue of deterioration when you hire lazy employees.

- **High flexibility level:** Pay attention to the level of flexibility of each employee you are planning to hire. It is so important to make sure all shifts get filled. The high level of flexibility of your employees will ensure this happens.

- **Understanding capability:** Strive to get team players who help minimize misunderstandings in the workplace. Failure to meet this working standard will ignite an uncomfortable working atmosphere that will chase away most of your good workers. Without a doubt, they will move to your competitors after leaving your business. This has to be the last mistake made in your business if you want to stay afloat and be profitable.

- **Good communicator:** Clear and attentive communication skills are needed, especially for the front and outside employees. They are the ones who greet customers, listen to and fulfill their needs. All this process will produce satisfactory results when you have workers with good communication skills, among other characteristics.

- **Profound integrity:** High level of integrity and authenticity are additional important traits you must be looking for while selecting your persuasive team of employees.

- **Culture cheerleaders:** If ethnicity is one of your business models, then feel free to recruit employees who can preserve and deliver that culture to the customers at full capacity. A good example is the Chinese and Indian restaurants. By the way, this is legal only if you can justify the merits behind your hiring process. Otherwise, it might backfire when you failed to execute it properly.

The list of the quality of employees to hire is not exhaustive. Let your business model and culture be your primary guidance while developing the useful list. In the end, you want to start a restaurant with employees who are capable to attract more customers you need. Moreover, to cover operating costs for your business and to generate sufficient profit.

## Source of hiring the right employees

Various resources can be deployed to assist you with the process of allocating the right people to work with you. Start with utilizing user-friendly and cost-effective employee allocation techniques before moving to the more costly ones. Some of the methods of getting staffs are:

- **Referral:** Word of mouth from your friends, relatives, winning team members, or coworkers is one of the cheapest and most effective tools to get the right candidates.

- **Social media:** Post your ad on social media including Craigslist, Facebook/Meta universe, and others. Some of them are free and they are so effective.

- **Newspaper:** If you think placing an ad in your local newspaper is an effective method to undertake, then utilize it. However, start by exploring the efficiency of the newspaper ad compared with the money you are planning to spend.

- **Location of business:** It is so common to see ads placed over the windows or doors in the front of the business buildings. Consider doing the same to save a lot of money and also to raise the level of awareness that your business will start operations soon.

- **Consultants:** Some recruiters are so effective when it comes to identifying the right candidates based on the characteristics offered by the employers and some are not. Effectively, use a winning equation to identify the right person to help with the recruiting exercise.

- **Radio ads:** Placing an ad on this media needs a proper assessment to evaluate between pros and cons of this method. The cost of placing an ad on the radio is huge. So, you have to do your homework right to avoid unexpected losses.

- **TV ads:** TV ads are the most effective way of getting many applicants, although it is not necessarily going to reach the right employees. It is very expensive for smaller business owners with limited cash to afford. So, you need to evaluate your budget very closely before you start burning your savings at the right investment but at the wrong time.

Utilize all possible legal options to get the right candidates. Some companies like Jackson Hewitt Company went the extra mile by hiring someone to dance and hold an ad sign in the road nearby, to persuade potential customers. Running a successful business is a matter of applying a high level of creativity, and logic, among others.

# How to pay restaurant employees

Let's start with employees who depend on tips to supplement their total wages, called *tipped employees*. According to the U.S. Department of Labor, the minimum wages for tipped employees in each state are indicated below.

## Minimum wages for tipped employees

| State | Basic combined cash and tip minimum wage rate ($) | Maximum tip credit against minimum wages ($) | Minimum cash wages ($) |
|---|---|---|---|
| Federal: Fair Labor Standards Acts (FLSA) | 7.25 | 5.12 | 2.13 |
| Alaska | | | 10.34 |
| California<br><br>• 25 employees or less<br>• 26 employees or more | | | 14<br><br>15 |
| Nevada | | | 9.75 |
| Washington | | | 14.49 |
| Florida | 10.00 | 3.02 | 6.98 |
| Hawaii | 10.10 | 0.75 | 9.35 |

| | | | |
|---|---|---|---|
| Idaho | 7.25 | 3.90 | 3.35 |
| Illinois | 12.00 | 4.80 | 7.20 |
| Iowa | 7.25 | 2.90 | 4.35 |
| Maine | 12.75 | 6.37 | 6.38 |
| New York | 13.20 | | |
| North Dakota | 7.25 | 2.39 | 4.86 |
| Virgin islands | 10.50 | 6.30 | 40% of 4.20 |
| Wisconsin | 8.75 | 70% of 6.13 | 2.62 |
| Alabama | | | 2.13 |
| Georgia | | | 2.13 |
| Indiana | 7.25 | 5.12 | 2.13 |
| Kansas | 7.25 | 5.12 | 2.13 |
| Kentucky | 7.25 | 5.12 | 2.13 |
| Minnesota<br><br>• Larger employer<br>• Small employer | | | 10.33<br><br>8.42 |
| Montana<br><br>• Over $100,000 sales<br>• $100,000 or less | | | 9.20<br><br><br>4.00 |
| Oregon | | | 12.75 |
| Arizona | 12.80 | 3.00 | 9.80 |

| Arkansas | 11.00 | 8.35 | 2.63 |
|---|---|---|---|
| Connecticut | 13.00 | | |
| Delaware | 10.50 | 8.27 | 2.23 |
| District of Colombia | 15.20 | 10.15 | 5.05 |
| Hawaii | 10.10 | 0.75 | 9.35 |
| Maine | 12.75 | 6.37 | 6.38 |
| Maryland | 12.50 | 8.87 | 3.63 |
| Massachusetts | 14.25 | 8.10 | 6.15 |
| Michigan | 9.87 | 6.12 | 3.75 |
| Missouri | 11.15 | 50% of 5.57 | 5.58 |
| New Hampshire | 7.25 | 55% 3.99 | 45% of 3.26 |
| New jersey | 13.00 | 7.87 | 5.13 |
| New Mexico | 11.50 | 8.70 | 2.80 |
| North Dakota | 7.25 | 33% of 2.39 | 4.86 |
| Ohio | 9.30 | 4.65 | 4.65 |
| Oklahoma | 7.25 | 5.12 | 2.13 |
| Pennsylvania | 7.25 | 4.42 | 2.83 |
| Rhode Island | 12.25 | 8.36 | 3.89 |
| South Dakota | 9.95 | 50% of 4.975 | 4.975 |

| | | | |
|---|---|---|---|
| Vermont | 12.55 | 6.27 | 6.28 |
| Louisiana | | | 2.13 |
| Mississippi | | | 2.13 |
| Nebraska | 9.00 | 6.87 | 2.13 |
| North Carolina | 7.25 | 5.12 | 2.13 |
| Puerto Rico | 8.50 | 6.37 | 2.13 |
| South Carolina | | | 2.13 |
| Tennessee | | | 2.13 |
| Texas | 7.25 | 5.12 | 2.13 |
| Utah | 7.25 | 5.12 | 2.13 |
| Virginia | 11.00 | 8.87 | 2.13 |
| Wyoming | 7.25 | 8.12 | 2.13 |

The chart indicates the minimum wages to pay your employees. Consider this as a bottom level you can start setting the wages from. To stay competitive in the labor market, you may need to pay them a little bit more than the minimum recommended amount. For the upper scale restaurants, the pay should be even better to stimulate morality and to retain good employees.

**Note:** Changes in the laws are happening constantly. Cross-check with your local state for the new up-to dates rates.

# Employees' background check

Unfortunately, your business will not be immune to bad employees, there are so many in the market. Unfortunately, some may fool you if necessary precautions are not executed in a timely fashion. Avoid accepting any employee just because you need one. You must have good staff with behavior that money cannot buy. A lot of employers pay a heavy price when untrustworthy employees start having problems that slow down business operations. They thought they were cutting corners to invest in the vetting procedure, which is a bad idea. Eventually, they end up dealing with tainted workers; sometimes, with criminal records.

# What is a background check?

This is a common process used in the hiring process by employers to verify their staff are who they say they are, they indeed possess those characteristics, experience, skills etc. Generally, the process covers things such as criminal records, employment history, bank account summary, and other relevant activities deemed necessary. The procedure can take as little as two days to say 30 or beyond depending on the extent of the vetting process.

# Benefits of doing the background check

There are plenty of benefits for business owners who decide to vet their employees before letting them sign contracts. Below are a few of the advantages of such checks ahead of time:

- **License check:** Just because someone did not get convicted, it does not imply that what he/she did is right such as possession of an incorrect social security card or driver's license.

- **Education background:** It helps to prove their level of education compared with what is shown on the application form.

- **Credit history:** You are advised to hire honest candidates to fill important positions such as a cashier or accountant. Some employers are vetting employees for these positions on their credit history to avoid fraud down the road.

- **Protection of property and other employees:** The outcomes of the vetting report also will allow you to isolate the criminals versus the good employees.

- **To determine the good characters:** You need this process to be done properly to maximize a degree of peace of mind for your property and the other employees working around.

- **Minimize turnover rate:** The process of changing workers often goes together with spending a lot of money to cover the procedure of looking for new employees. Try to use this report wisely in selecting stable employees who have a higher chance of staying longer.

The process of vetting has to be done professionally with the full consent of the prospective employee. Prospects have to fill out the form, sign, and date it, allowing you to move forward with the vetting process. Remember, it is illegal to sneak behind the prospects back to perform background checks without proper permission.

When you are ready to vet someone, there are a lot of companies that can do this process on your behalf. The fees associated with vetting services start as low as $15 to $500. The range is so wide that it requires you to do some level of research before requesting one.

# Dealing with fake vetting schemes

The benefits of conducting a good and fair background check to the business owners are many. However, the outcomes of this process will only produce the intended outcome if all parties play their roles. Unfortunately, many prospective employees run a Ponzi scheme trying to do whatever it takes to scam their employers. Below are some of the tricks the scammers are using against employers:

- They like to challenge the necessity and accuracy of the vetting process and its outcomes.
- They pretend to be living with the other family members because they do not want employers to run any previous working history.
- Some do volunteer to provide their vetting report.
- They also use fake references and addresses in their application forms.
- They tell you that they are ready to start working immediately.

The vetting process will be just a waste of time.
You definitely do not want to be the next person in line to be scammed. Take enough time to prepare a detailed plan of how you will be dealing with bad employees in an attempt of getting the right ones.

Employees have a direct and powerful ability to derail your business if proper care in selecting them is not followed. This book has analyzed a lot of important things that you need to execute to get the right staff, who are willing to work and be productive enough to maximize ROI. When the process of either identifying or recruiting them becomes much tougher on your side, you can hire someone with enough experience to handle the task much faster and in a creative manner.

The process of getting the right candidates who are willing to work with you might look complicated and time-consuming. However, when all necessary procedures for recruiting them are followed, the results are worth the effort. Since the rate of productivity in your work place depends on many factors, including having a good team of employees; all efforts to treat them right should be implemented and followed accordingly. Make sure your business model comprises a comprehensive plan for maximizing employees' satisfaction rates such as good pay rates, inclusive shifts, considerable working hours, and others.

Follow the U.S. Department of Labor and your local state guidelines when setting the wage rates of your workers. When you allow workers to work overtime, make sure they are getting paid based on the requirements, which is one hour and half of the regular pay. Practicing how to treat employees in the right way should be in the culture of your business. Once you succeed to implement the right culture in your business, it facilitates to increase the morality of your employees, retention rate and cut down operation expenses, just to name a few. All these positive outcomes are so beneficial to your business because they are the main contributor to either getting a positive or negative ROI.

# To-Do List Form – Chapter Five

| Action | Goals | Results(Y/N) |
|---|---|---|
| **Time-sensitive actions:**<br><br>1.<br><br>2.<br><br>3.<br><br>4.<br><br>5.<br><br>6.<br><br>7.<br><br>8.<br><br>9.<br><br>10. | | |
| **Less time-sensitive actions**<br><br>1.<br><br>2.<br><br>3.<br><br>4. | | |

| 5. | | |
| 6. | | |
| 7. | | |
| 8. | | |
| 9. | | |
| 10. | | |

# Read Again Pages – Chapter Five

| Page # | Topic/Subtopic | Purpose | Result (Y/N) |
|---|---|---|---|
|  |  |  |  |
|  |  |  |  |
|  |  |  |  |
|  |  |  |  |
|  |  |  |  |

# Chapter Six

## Acquisition, storage, and control of supply

In addition to spending a big chunk of money on payroll expenses, also expect to be dealing with another complicated task of acquiring foodstuffs and supplies. When produce and supplies are acquired, additional procedures should be put in place to store them in a safe and satisfactory place. Once the consumption time comes, all inventory control processes must be prepared ahead of time and be followed accordingly to ensure proper allocation of each item leaving the storage room. Before moving forward, let us look at the basic definitions of foodstuff and supply.

### Definition of supply

Supply is defined as the collective amount of goods or services that have been set aside for consumption. The Merriam-Webster website defines supply as the quantity or amount of a commodity needed or available for consumption. Also, it comprises the quantities of goods or services offered for sale at a particular time and at a given price.

**Definition of foodstuff**

According to the Merriam-Webster dictionary, foodstuff is defined as the raw material of food before or after processing.

Based on the above definitions of supply and foodstuff, the word supply also includes foodstuff. From now onwards, I will drop foodstuff from the explanations and just use supply only.

The discussion of this topic will cover both types of suppliers, which are perishable items such as food and non-perishable items that comprise things such as toilet paper, utensils, and cleaning materials, among others. In summary form, there are three primary components of dealing with suppliers that are happening in many businesses, including the restaurant industry. The process starts by acquiring supplies from the vendor, finding the proper place to store them, and finally, controlling the usage process.

**The equation for appropriate supply management**

**Appropriate supply management = Acquisition procedure + Storage process + Inventory control**

Each step above is very important and requires comprehensive and functional planning procedures before executing it. The entire process of dealing with suppliers will produce positive outcomes when all three processes are handled properly. Neither one is better than the other, all of them carry constant weight on the degree of importance when it comes to measuring the cost savings and the productivity level of each one.

# Supply acquisition

Before you start looking for places to purchase the food and other items for your business, you must prepare the budget first. A budget is comprised of projections of revenue and expenses in a given period. Since the discussion is not focusing on the budget of the entire restaurant, the component of revenue will be eliminated from the definition for now. Suppliers you need in your business should be prepared with consideration of various factors including:

- **Total customers:** Projected number of customers to allow for a given time frame must be known. For clarity purposes, allocate this figure on weekly basis followed by monthly, and so on. This figure is so important in reaching the correct and functional budget. Therefore, it must be supported with the searched data and practical assumptions when possible.

- **Type of menu:** The list of menus you will serve is so important to understand the big picture of what type of food you need. In the beginning, you can start with a few, but important dishes before moving to the second phase with additional new dishes. Periodically, the process can proceed until all menus get filled up.

- **Number of menus:** Some restaurants have different menus for lunch and dinner. Some just switch some of the menus and retain others for both shifts. No matter the size of each dish, all menus must be accounted for to get the correct estimates.

- **Vendor:** Make a shortlist of vendors that you prefer to enter into a contract with as primary sources of your food supplies. The plan also should focus on where to get nonperishable suppliers. Consider signing with the wholesale providers such as Restaurant Depot, Sam's Club, Costco, and others in order to get a lot of supplies at a cheap price.

- **Frequency:** Assess the size of your storage room and daily consumption to understand how many times a week the vendor needs to deliver the food and other stuff. Remember, you need to have the right balance between understock and overstock to stay profitable.

Bring all these details to the table while preparing the budget to simplify the whole process of reaching accurate estimates. The more detailed and accurate you are, the higher the chance of getting a useful and cost-effective budget. With no doubt, ask for help when the needs arise. It is better to wait for a few days to get help from a professional rather than rushing to prepare a nonfunctional budget. When you choose this route, prepare to spend a few hundred dollars to get valuable input on this critical budget preparation process. The final budget is supposed to be as accurate as possible to reflect the true picture of your business operations. The presence of large variation between the actual and budgeted expenditures is not recommended. Once this happens, necessary correction measures should be applied in a timely fashion to avoid further damage to your balance sheet.

Moreover, for all suppliers that are not delivered to the building by the vendor, proper transportation measures should be put in place ahead of time. Whether you buy a van, a pickup, or just be using a rental, the bottom line is, you need to have a reliable and cost-effective means of transport. Failure to arrange this crucial means of transport could cause delays to important supplies. Which in turn, will affect the completeness of your menus or total quality of service to your customers. Generally, your operations will be shaky and unsatisfactory. And you will start getting bad reviews, which will destroy your business reputation.

# Type of vendor to choose

Various food supplier vendors exist in the market. Some are operating in a few states or geographical areas and others have enough manpower to operate nationwide. Below is the list of a few vendors that you may consider contacting:

**List of food vendor**

1. **SYSCO**
   Contact:        281-584-1390
   Headquarters:   Houston, TX
   Regions:        Nationwide
   Website:        www.sysco.com

2. **U.S. FOODS**
   Contact:        847-720-8000
   Headquarters:   Rosemont, IL
   Regions:        Nationwide
   Website:        www.usfoods.com

3. **MCLANE FOOD SERVICE**
   Contact:        972-364-2052
   Headquarters:   Temple, TX
   Regions:        Nationwide
   Website:        www.mclaneco.com

4. **PERFORMANCE FOOD SERVICE**
   Contact:        (804) 484-7700
   Headquarters:   Richmond, VA
   Regions:        Nationwide
   Tractors:       2,047
   Website:        www.performancefoodservice.com

5. **GORDON FOOD SERVICE**
   Contact:        (888) 437-3663
   Headquarters:   Wyoming, MI
   Regions:        Nationwide
   Website:        www.gfs.com/en-us

6. **REINHART FOOD SERVICE**
   Contact:        (800) 332-8170
   Headquarters:   Chicago, IL
   Regions:        Nationwide
   Website:        www.rfsdelivers.com

7. **THE MARTIN-BROWER CO.**
   Contact:        (618) 537-6121
   Headquarters:   IL
   Regions:        Nationwide
   Website:        www.martinbrower.us

8. **DOT TRANSPORTATION**
   Contact:        877-368-4968
   Headquarters:   Mt. Sterling, IL
   Regions:        Nationwide
   Website:        www.drivefordot.com

9. **BEN E. KEITH CO.**
   Contact:        (817) 759-6000
   Headquarters:   Fort Worth, TX
   Regions:        Nationwide
   Website:        www.benekeith.com

10. **GOLDEN STATE FOODS**
    Contact:        949-247-8000
    Headquarters:   Irvine, CA
    Regions:        Nationwide
    Website:        www.goldenstatefoods.com

## 11. SHAMROCK FOODS CO.
Contact:        (602) 233-6400
Headquarters:   Phoenix, AZ
Regions:        Nationwide
Website:        www.shamrockfoodservice.com

## 12. KEHE DISTRIBUTORS
Contact:        (812) 333-1511
Headquarters:   Naperville, IL
Regions:        Nationwide
Website:        www.kehe.com

## 13. PFG CUSTOMIZED
Contact:        (803) 366-6399
Headquarters:   Lebanon, TN
Regions:        Nationwide
Website:        www.pfgcdc.com

## 14. VISTAR TRANSPORTATION
Contact:        (800) 880-9900
Headquarters:   Englewood, CO
Regions:        Nationwide
Website         www.vistar.com

## 15. BUFFALO ROCK CO.
Contact:        (205) 940-9799
Headquarters:   Birmingham, AL
Regions:        Nationwide
Website:        www.buffalorock.com

# Additional list of food vendor

Other food distributors are mentioned below:
- Labatt Food Service
- Blue Line Foodservice Distribution
- Perdue Transportation Inc.
- Lipari Foods
- Trans Papa Logistics
- Artic Glacier USA
- QuikTrip Distribution
- Blue Bell Creameries
- Dutch Valley
- Coastal Pacific Food Distributors
- DPI Specialty Foods
- Utz Quality Foods
- Golden State Snack Foods
- Jake's Finer Foods
- Vendors Supply Inc.

Although the list looks long, it is not exhaustive. There are a lot of local distributors who offer competitive prices closer or the same as the big vendors. Some of them also carry a wider range of varieties that might suit the needs of your business model. Spend extra time exploring the list of vendors who are cheap, liable, and offer many varieties. Pick the one that you think understands and would be willing to fulfill your short and long-term goals of supplies you need. Ultimately, food acquisition is one of the more important segments of restaurant operations that you should not avoid.

## Key characteristics of the right vendor to look for

While looking for the list of vendors or distributors to be a major source of your food supply, try to narrow down the key characteristics of the right candidates. Your list should be broad to touch on all major issues, such as:

- **Price:** Pay attention to their price practices. Look for the availability of any offers or discounts. Do not forget to justify the quality of supplies and the service they offer in relation to the price they charge.

- **Coverage:** Just because the vendor operates nationwide does not mean they carry all types of foods or stuff you need. Whether you are exploring the regional or nationwide vendor, make sure the right candidate meets your needs.

- **One-stop shopping:** The more supplies you get from one vendor the higher the chance of securing good deals. You will also save on transportation costs for your business.

- **Minimum purchase:** Some vendors have a minimum order limit to qualify or to retain your membership status. Try to assess their requirements ahead of time to avoid service disruption at a critical time.

- **Availability:** With the exclusion of the public holidays, some vendors are open every day and for extended hours. So, compare your schedule and theirs to pick the one that will not affect the general operations of your business.

- **Membership:** Some of the distributors have a membership service that you need to join for their services. Make sure you read all the fine print before you sign the contract. Some of the lines in these contracts might carry tough restrictions that might jeopardize the operations of your business down the road.

- **Value-added services:** After becoming a member, some vendors offer additional benefits that differ from one company to another. Stay vigilant in this crucial area of saving money.

- **Quality:** The food industry is one of the most competitive businesses so you cannot offer substandard dishes. Just because you want to save some costs does not mean you have to buy low-quality supplies. If you do, you could lose valuable customers that you worked very hard to retain. This and other shortcuts will open the door for your competitors to steal your business much sooner beyond your projections.

There are a huge number of benefits offered by these vendors. These benefits differ from one vendor to another. To get the best deal, explore the incentives they offer before choosing the right vendor who complements your business model. Price alone should not be a decisive factor. Consider utilizing other essential influences mentioned above as a starting point.

**Techniques of negotiating the price for inventories**

In the business world, there is always room for negotiations. You must possess high skills in spotting the opportunities and knowing how to go about them for your benefit. Of course, you need to brush up on the skill of being a good negotiator. Once you master it, it will help you secure many deals ahead of your rivals. Remember, the success of your business relies on many factors, including your ability to seek, negotiate, and win many deals in a timely fashion.

Before you start initiating conversations with vendors, practice various winning scenarios to guarantee the maximum degree of success. Some of the scenario techniques are detailed below:

- Have detailed preparations that cover the entire list of negotiations.
- Avoid lying in any documents or other types of communications.
- Prove your level of potential to justify the favor you are looking for. They need to see a win-win scenario for both parties.
- Make convincing arguments to justify the importance of listening to your reasoning and using their rivals as justifiable factors.
- Since both sides will be fighting to be winners, know how to spot a fair compromise.

- Consider the advantages of long-term goals to the business in these negotiations ahead of the short-term goals.
- Avoid using force as a negotiating technique. It never produces positive results.
- To simplify the progress and for future reference, start the procedure in writing.

From the points above, maximize these ideas by

- Having enough practice
- Conduct intensive drills, and
- Adopt practical rehearsal before the first day of the meeting.

As always, you cannot beat the power of having state of the art preparations in any project management. Remember, most of the time the other side will offer you only one chance to prove your point. The outcomes of the negotiations will make you either a winner or a loser. Make sure you do not allow failure to prevail ahead of you just because you did not take this process very seriously. Always, try to prepare yourself well to secure the jackpots in all trials.

**Storage process**

Now you have food on the doorstep of your restaurant. The next step is to find a decent place to store it while waiting for the consumption date and time. Generally, perishable food requires closer attention to preserve the maximum level of freshness. It starts from the time you purchase or receive from the vendor's truck to the storage place, preparation procedures, and cooking techniques; before being served to the customer. In each step of movement, prepare inclusive and sound procedures for protecting the quality of the food. Also, these procedures should take into consideration, various ways of maximizing the life span of the food.

Extend your research to include the city guidelines on how to deal with food in all mentioned steps above. The US Food and Drug Administration (FDA) set various codes for handling food including storing them at least six inches above the floor. Some state and local governments prefer at least a foot above the floor.

Various methods of food storage can be utilized as long as they fit within the guidelines of your local food safety department. Four of the most basic storage places are:

- Dry staples
- Freeze-dried
- Dehydrated
- Canned

## Basic principles of safe food storage

As you are trying to draw a clear line between the safety of the food and the total expenses of supplies, you better adopt enhanced practices that will benefit both sides. Come up with a useful list that is simple but effective to follow. If training is the last resort for your employees to master these principles, then consider preparing functional training sessions using an experienced tutor to deliver the message. Below are some of the safety techniques to supplement your list of safe food storage:

- **Cleanness**: You must make sure the entire storage places are clean, including the floor, at all times. All the shelves and racks also must not be contaminated in anyway. The cleaning schedule should be prepared and followed at all times.

- **Food separation:** Do not allow any contact between foods; mostly, raw food and cooked foods.

- **Temperatures:** Follow the recommendations of the city codes while regulating the temperature of foods in your restaurant. Consider incorporating it with the manufacturer or producer guidelines to achieve maximum results.

- **Positioning:** Food must be placed logically to avoid spoilage. For instance, you cannot put heavy stuff on veggies or fruits.

- **Air contamination:** For foods that need to be placed in sealed plastic or containers, the process should be done carefully to avoid air penetration. Remember, oxygen is a primary contributor to food deterioration. Try to play safe to minimize food wastage.

- **Distance:** You are not allowed to store food on the floor. Follow the codes of your city regarding the distance required from one type of food to another.

- **Disposal:** With no hesitance, discard the spoiled food right away to protect unaffected batches. Also, it helps eliminate bacteria from reaching the customers.

- **Washing hands:** The procedure of washing hands should also be extended to the food handlers in addition to cookers or savers. All employees should understand the benefits and the necessity of washing hands regularly and after using the bathroom. When the efforts of the compliance produce unsatisfactory results, then you can place the hands washing signs in all primary spots such as the kitchen, bathroom, storage room, and others.

- **Functionality:** All storage places such as deep freezers, industrial refrigerators, racks, and shelves, among others must be in a good condition. Moreover, they should be working properly and receive periodic repairs as recommended by the manufacturer. The repair technician should be certified to work on a particular type of storage equipment.

Despite having a code of ethics to guide you with all processes of dealing with food that starts when you receive the food to the last step of saving to the customers, still, you must go above and beyond those rules. You have to understand that those who will be eating your food are human beings the same as your loved ones. You are highly encouraged to start by using common sense to a wider degree before even thinking about the city guidelines. Let these guidelines be a supplemental tool in addition to what you have prepared in your business plan.

When you have questions about food handling procedures, you may contact the food safety department in your state. The information is indicated in the following page:

**List of Department of Food Safety and Hygiene in your state**

| State | Department |
|---|---|
| Kansas | The Kansas Department of Agriculture: Food Safety and Loading<br><br>https://agriculture.ks.gov/divisions-programs/food-safety-lodging |
| Georgia | Georgia Department of Public Health: Food Safety<br><br>https://dph.georgia.gov/environmental-health/food-service |
| DC | Food Safety and Hygiene Inspection Services Division<br><br>The Food Safety and Hygiene Inspection Services Division |

| | |
|---|---|
| Missouri | Missouri Department of Health and Senior Services (DHSS) and local public health agencies (LPHA). |
| Virgin Islands | The Virgin Islands Department of Health, Division of Environmental Health |
| West Virginia | The Public Health Sanitation Division of the Bureau for Public Health 304-558-2981, https://oehs.wvdhhr.org/phs/food-safety |
| Alabama | Alabama Public Health<br><br>https://dph.georgia.gov/environmental-health/food-service |
| Indiana | Indiana Department of Health: Food Protection Division<br><br>https://www.in.gov/health/food-protection/ |
| Kentucky | Kentucky Cabinet for Health and Family Services: Food Safety Branch<br><br>https://chfs.ky.gov/ |
| Alaska | Division of Environmental Health: Food Safety and Sanitation Program<br><br>https://dec.alaska.gov/eh/fss.aspx |
| North Dakota | North Dakota Health Food and Loading<br><br>https://www.health.nd.gov/regulation-licensure/food-and-lodging |

| | |
|---|---|
| New York | New York State Department of Health |
| | https://www.health.ny.gov/environmental/ind oors/food_safety/ |
| Florida | Florida Health: Food Safety and Sanitation |
| | https://www.floridahealth.gov/environmental-health/food-safety-and-sanitation/index.html |
| Hawaii | State of Hawaii: Department of Health Food Safety Branch |
| | https://health.hawaii.gov/san/ |
| Illinois | Illinois Department of Public Health |
| | https://dph.illinois.gov/topics-services/food-safety.html |
| Iowa | Iowa Department of Public Health |
| | https://idph.iowa.gov/ |
| Maine | Maine Division of Environmental and Community Health |
| | https://www.maine.gov/dhhs/mecdc/environm ental-health/el/index.htm |
| Nevada | Nevada Division of Public and Behavioral Health |
| | https://agri.nv.gov/Food/Food_Safety/Food_S afety_Home/ |
| Oregon | Oregon Health Authority: Food Safety |

| | |
|---|---|
| | https://www.oregon.gov/oha/ph/healthyenviro nments/foodsafety/pages/foodcode.aspx |
| Washington | Washington State Department of Health: Food safety |
| | https://doh.wa.gov/community-and-environment/food/food-worker-and-industry/food-safety-rules |
| Montana | Montana Department of Health and Human Services: Food and Consumer Safety |
| | https://dphhs.mt.gov/publichealth/FCSS/Retai lFood/ |
| South Dakota | South Dakota Department of Health: Food and Lodging Safety |
| | https://doh.sd.gov/food/restaurants-lodging/operators.aspx |
| California | California Department of Public Health: Food and Drug Branch |
| | https://www.cdfa.ca.gov/ahfss/Animal_Health /Food_Safety.html |
| North Carolina | North Carolina Department of Health and Human Services: Food Protection Program |
| | https://www.ncagr.gov/fooddrug/foodsafety/ |
| Oklahoma | Oklahoma State Department of Health: Food Service |

https://ag.ok.gov/divisions/food-safety/

| | |
|---|---|
| Mississippi | Mississippi State Department of Health |
| | https://msdh.ms.gov/msdhsite/_static/43,0,37 7.html |
| Delaware | The Office of Food Protection (OFP) |
| | https://www.dhss.delaware.gov/dhss/dph/hsp/ foodsafety.html |
| Massachusetts | Massachusetts Department of Food Safety |
| | https://www.mass.gov/food-safety |
| Ohio | Ohio Department of Health |
| | https://odh.ohio.gov/know-our-programs/food-safety-program |
| Minnesota | Minnesota Department of Health: Food Safety |
| | https://www.health.state.mn.us/people/foodsa fety/ |
| Utah | Utah Department of Health: Food Safety |
| | https://health.utah.gov/hepatitisa/food-safety |
| Arizona | Arizona Department of Health Services: Food Safety and Environmental Services |
| | https://www.azdhs.gov/preparedness/epidemi ology-disease-control/food-safety-environmental-services/index.php#school-garden-program-home |

| | |
|---|---|
| New Mexico | New Mexico Department of Food Safety Bureau |
| | https://www.env.nm.gov/foodprogram/ |
| Nebraska | Nebraska Food Safety and Consumer Protection |
| | https://nda.nebraska.gov/fscp/foods/food_safety |
| Tennessee | Tennessee Department of Food safety |
| | https://www.tn.gov/health/cedep/environmental/healthy-places/healthy-places/healthy-buildings/hb/tennessee-healthy-meetings-guidelines/food-safety.html |
| Indiana | Indiana Department of Health: Food Protection Division |
| | https://www.in.gov/health/food-protection/ |
| New Jersey | New Jersey Department of Health: Consumer Food Safety |
| | https://www.nj.gov/health/ceohs/phfpp/retailfood/ |
| Colorado | Colorado Department of Public Health and Environment: Food Regulations |
| | https://cdphe.colorado.gov/food-safety-and-licensing |
| Pennsylvania | Pennsylvania Department of Food Safety |

| | |
|---|---|
| | https://www.agriculture.pa.gov/consumer_protection/FoodSafety/retail-food-inspection-reports/pages/default.aspx |
| South Carolina | South Carolina Department of Health and Environmental Control: Food Safety |
| | https://scdhec.gov/food-safety |
| Maryland | Maryland Department of Health: Food Protection |
| | https://health.maryland.gov/phpa/OEHFP/OFPCHS/pages/home.aspx |
| Louisiana | Louisiana Department of Health |
| | https://ldh.la.gov/page/656 |
| Rhode Island | State of Rhode Island: Food Safety |
| | https://health.ri.gov/food/ |
| Connecticut | Connecticut Department of Public Health |
| | https://portal.ct.gov/dph/Food-Protection-Program/Main-Page |
| Wyoming | Wyoming Department of Health: Food Safety |
| | https://health.wyo.gov/publichealth/infectious-disease-epidemiology-unit/food-safety/ |
| Arkansas | Arkansas Department of Health: Food Protection |
| | https://www.healthy.arkansas.gov/programs- |

| | |
|---|---|
| | services/topics/food-protection |
| Idaho | Idaho Department of Health and Welfare: Food Safety |
| | https://healthandwelfare.idaho.gov/health |
| Michigan | Michigan Department of Health: Food Safety |
| | https://www.michigan.gov/mde/services/food/sntp/resources/food-safety |
| Virginia | Virginia Department of Health |
| | https://www.vdh.virginia.gov/environmental-health/food-safety-in-virginia/ |
| New Hampshire | New Hampshire Department of Health: Food Protection |
| | https://www.dhhs.nh.gov/programs-services/environmental-health-and-you/food-protection |
| Vermont | Vermont Department of Health and Environment: Food Protection |
| | https://www.healthvermont.gov/environment/food-lodging/food-safety-consumers |
| Wisconsin | Wisconsin Department of Health Services: Food Safety |
| | https://www.dhs.wisconsin.gov/nutrition/safety.htm |

Try to build a culture that loves to play a safe game instead of doing it just to please the city personnel. Once you managed to build that safety culture for your employees, the concept of practice safety in your business will start to look much easier compared to many restaurant owners who are constantly struggling in this arena. Build a practical foundation that understands the importance of running a business with a long-term vision. Without a doubt, these visions will be attained much faster once you put the interest of the customer first ahead of the profit.

## Inventory control

The importance of receiving and storing supplies alone will not give you sufficient outcomes when you neglect the consumption process. You have to come up with sound procedures for supervising the way inventories are taken out of the storage places.

### Inventory management

In the restaurant industry, inventory management is defined as the combined process of ordering the supplies, storing, and using them. The reasons for caring for this process are many including:

- Keeping enough food and ingredients to meet the need of the customers at a specified period.
- Another benefit is to minimize and possibly eliminate spoilage and theft of inventories.

In the beginning, you may start by conducting the inventory process manually to save some money. If you do, try to develop a spreadsheet that possesses primary columns to suit your needs. Below are some of the columns and headers that you might find useful to start developing your spreadsheet.

# Sample: Inventory Receipt, Storage, and Usage Report

## Business Name

**Goods Receiving Form**

| | |
|---|---|
| No | : |
| Supplier Code | : |
| Supplier Name | : |
| DO Code | : |
| DO Date | : |
| Address | : |
| Telephone | : |
| Contact Person | : |

| No | Item Code | Item Name | UOM | Qty | Unit Price | Amount |
|---|---|---|---|---|---|---|
| | | | | | | |
| | | | | | | |
| | | | | | | |
| | | | | | | |
| | | | | | | |
| | | | | | | |
| | | | | | | |
| | | | | | | |
| | | | | | | |
| | | | | | | |
| | | | | | | |
| | | | | | | |
| | | | | | | |
| | | | | | | |
| | | | | | | |
| | | | | | | |
| | | | | | | |
| | | | | | Total | |

Checked by:          Date:          Signature:

Approved by:        Date:          Signature:

When your business starts to grow, then you may consider purchasing software to simplify this process. There are a great number of suitable software packages in the market that meet the needs of customers of all sizes and budgets. Start by evaluating your needs before you start searching for which software to purchase. Below is the list of some of the inventory-related software your business might benefit with:

- **MarketMan:** It has been evaluated as the best overall inventory software by many users.

- **XtraChef by Toast:** It is user friendly including toast point of sale (POS) integration.

- **Upserve by Lightspeed:** It works well in the automation ordering process.

- **CrunchTime:** Best for restaurants with many branches. Also, those that need to conduct labor cost analysis constantly.

- **Revel Systems:** This software is ideal when security is your number one issue.

# Adoption of the FIFO rule

This is one of the accounting rules, particularly in inventory management that helps to control the usage of suppliers. FIFO stands for "first in first out". It means the first inventory to arrive in the warehouse or storage room, must be the first item to be taken out or consumed. When this concept is in operation, it helps to ensure that older products are consumed first ahead of the newer ones. It helps to deal with the issue of letting suppliers sit so long in the storage room without being used to the point of passing the expiration dates.

## Benefits of the FIFO rule

This inventory management system has plenty of benefits that most business owners will find useful to explore. Some of these advantages are listed below:

- **Warranty control:** Since the supplies do not sit for so long in the storage room, those that possess the manufacturer warrant will not be affected.

- **Quality control**: The shorter the inventory stays in the storeroom, the higher the chance to preserve the quality of items.

- **Simplify storage operations:** It allows the inventory to be stored in an orderly manner and helps the entire process of receiving, storing, and dispatching the inventories.

- **It reflects the current inventory figure:** Having only newer products in the store gives the ending inventory a current market value, which is so useful in the cost management and budgeting process.

- **Lower inventory cost:** This rule minimizes the occurrences of spoilage, which is the main contributor to inventory losses.

These and other advantages of adopting the FIFO rule in your business are powerful and have a higher possibility of maximizing ROI. To stay ahead of your competitors; constantly, build a habit of exploring new methods of improving the general performance of your business. Once you allocate one, try to learn how to use it before you initiate functional training for your employees promptly. The faster you become in allocating and implementing new methods in your business, the less the operational turbulences your business will experience. When you managed to implement a system that guarantees smooth business operations, the more profitable your business will become.

The entire process of dealing with inventory is wider, more sensitive, and time-consuming. However, most prospective owners are taking it for granted. The route starts by allocating the right stuff to purchase and choosing the right vendors to suit the needs of your business. Others are the delivery process, having functional storage procedures, and the consumption process.

For your business to stay competitive, you must develop an inclusive and useful plan for each step and conduct enough tests to assess the functionality and productivity level. Only those plans that managed to pass the highest score can be implemented in your business operations. Those that are less satisfactory, try to find other options for improving them before inserting them into the line of operations.

## To-Do List Form – Chapter Six

| Action | Goals | Results(Y/N) |
|---|---|---|
| **Time-sensitive actions:**<br><br>1.<br><br>2.<br><br>3.<br><br>4.<br><br>5.<br><br>6.<br><br>7.<br><br>8.<br><br>9.<br><br>10. | | |
| **Less time-sensitive actions**<br><br>1.<br><br>2.<br><br>3.<br><br>4. | | |

| | | |
|---|---|---|
| 5. | | |
| 6. | | |
| 7. | | |
| 8. | | |
| 9. | | |
| 10. | | |

# Read Again Pages – Chapter Six

| Page # | Topic/Subtopic | Purpose | Result (Y/N) |
|---|---|---|---|
|  |  |  |  |
|  |  |  |  |
|  |  |  |  |
|  |  |  |  |
|  |  |  |  |

# Chapter Seven

## Running a sound financial system for your business

Running a successful business goes hand-in-hand with understanding the purposeful movement of money in your business in both directions. The process of allocating incoming funds, known as revenue, should be monitored closely. In the same way, pay closer attention to the outgoing income, which represents the total expenditure. A good financial system in your business should be able to:

- Efficiently allocating resources.
- Assessing and managing financial risks.
- Allocate all transactions in a timely fashion.
- Immediately, detect any irregularities or any form of fraud.
- Prevent occurrences of fraud from happening.
- Reveal a big picture of the financial soundness of your business.

- Help in decision-making using various types of ratios.
- Ensure availability of adequate resources of the fund as needed.

Even though you are planning to hire an accountant to handle all business needs, it is still a wise idea to take the initiative to learn about the accounting field. Try to maintain a basic knowledge that will allow you to understand initial signs when things start going wrong. One of the primary duties of accountants is to monitor the financial aspects of their clients. However, they will not be there with a warning message regarding the deterioration or occurrences of something harmful to their businesses. Experience shows that operating a business this way does not favor owners most of the time.

It is even worse when the accountant experiences problems without your knowledge. Sometimes, it happens when the accountant starts running behind due to many factors, including lack of integrity and having too many customers compared with the available resources, among other things. At this point, your business will become a victim. Please do not be solely depending on one person you cannot control all the time. Now the question is: how soon will you detect the problem if it is happening? Is it after the damage is beyond your ability to handle it? Or will you wait until the size of the destruction is too big to force you to shut down your business?

The above questions are very important to ask yourself and come up with alternative solutions before waiting to be a primary target. You are the owner of a business that empowers you to be the primary guide. Try to understand both the primary and secondary functions of your CEO position and work diligently to fulfill them accordingly. Any time you start experiencing limitations either of managerial ability or lack of time to manage your business, you better seek assistance right away before your business starts derailing and losing customers.

The bottom line is you need to maintain a high level of self-awareness in each aspect of your business. This means you have to be ahead of the game rather than operating a business like an interloper.

## Understanding basic financial knowledge

Technically, it is so hard to replace the position of an accountant if you do not possess that knowledge. Still, the advantages of speaking the same language with him/her are unreplaceable. It means you must have the ability to understand at least the basic idea of a few accounting terminologies required to comprehend the financial report when presented to you. Below is a list of a few basic accounting terminologies that should be able to understand:

- **Accounts payable**: It includes the list of all business expenses incurred in a given period, but the payments have not been done yet. The total figure goes to the balance sheet as a liability.
- **Accounts receivable**: It includes the list of all business revenue incurred in a given period, but the payments have not been collected yet. The total figure goes to the balance sheet as an asset.
- **Accrued expenses:** It occurs when an expense transaction took place without being paid.
- **Asset:** It comprises the list of all anything in business possession that has a monetary value.
- **Liability:** It includes the list of all business debts that have not been settled yet.
- **Balance sheet:** It is part of the business financial statement that comprises all assets, liabilities, and owners' equity.

**Mathematically**
The balance sheet equation is:
**Assets = Liabilities + Owners' Equity**

- **Book value:** This is the original value of the asset at the time it was put in business or purchased for business uses. Periodically, all assets do get depreciated. To get the current value of an asset you have to take the book value less accumulated depreciation.

**Mathematically**

The book value equation is:

**Current value = book value – accumulated depreciation**

**Then**

**Book value = current value – accumulated depreciation**

- **Owners' Equity:** This is the total amount of the value of the business that belongs to the owners of the business.

**Mathematically**

The Owners' Equity value is calculated by taking:

**Owners' Equity = total assets - total liabilities**

- **Inventory:** It includes all assets purchased by the business for sale. In the restaurant industry, food is a good example of inventory.
- **Depreciation:** It comprises the value of the asset that is lost over time due to its usability. Remember, not all assets are depreciable. Examples of depreciable assets are equipment and a car, among others.
- **Expenses:** It comprises a list of costs incurred by the business during the formation and operations times.
- **Gross margin:** It is a section of the business profitability after deducting the cost of goods sold.

**Mathematically:**
**Gross margin = (Revenue – Cost of goods sold) / Revenue**

- **Gross profit:** It is a section of the business profitability before deducting total business operating expenses.
- **The income statement:** Sometimes it is known as a *Statement of Profit and Loss*. It is a statement that shows business revenue, expenses, and profit/loss for a given period.
- **Net income:** It is a positive result that occurred after taking business total revenue less cost of goods sold, total operating expenses, depreciation, and taxes.
- **Net loss:** It is a negative result that occurred after taking business total revenue less cost of goods sold, total operating expenses, depreciation, and taxes.
- **Revenue:** It comprises all money earned during business operations.
- **Cash flow:** It shows the inflows and outflows of cash at a given period.
- **Positive cash flow** means the business has accumulated more cash than what it spent in a given period.
- **Negative cash flow** means the business has accumulated less cash than what it spent in a given period.
- **Credit:** It is a business situation that occurs when there is an increase in liability, owner's equity, or decrease in an asset or expenses.
- **Debit:** It is a business situation that occurs when there is an increase in an asset or expenses or a decrease in liability, owner's equity.
- **Fixed cost:** It comprises all business expenses that do not change due to the increase or decrease in sales. Examples of fixed costs are rent, loan payment, insurance, license fees, and salaries.
- **Variable cost:** It comprises all business expenses that do change due to the increase or decrease of sales. Examples of variable costs are cooking gas, hourly wages, and food.

Let your educational background lead you while deciding the length of the list of the terminologies you need. If you find yourself getting confused about understanding this accounting jargon, you may set it aside. Alternatively, find a reliable and committed accountant that will be the backbone of your business in this field.

## Break-even analysis

A break-even analysis is a financial calculation that balances the business operation expenses or product against the number of units sold or services delivered in a dollar figure. In other words, it shows the number of units or amount of services to be sold to cover total expenses before you start making a profit.

**Sample: Break-even chart**

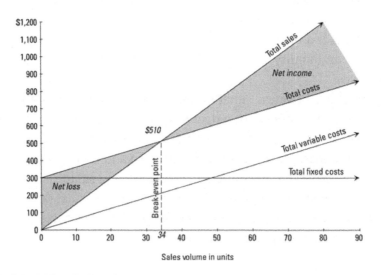

Based on the example break-even chart above, it implies that your business will start making a profit when you managed to sell 34 plates of the particular food daily.

**Formulas for calculating the break-even**

**Formula**

> Break-Even Point (sales dollars) = Fixed Costs ÷ Contribution Margin.
> Contribution Margin = Price of Product – Variable Costs

**Benefits of a break-even analysis**

Normally how many plates to sell a day before you start making a profit is a propounding experience you do not want to miss. The knowledge facilitates business owners to evaluate their strategies to see if they are productive or not. Additional benefits are mentioned below:

- **Starting capital:** The figure helps you to understand how much starting and working capital you need before you start your business. If your business starts making a profit after five months, then you have to figure out how the bills will be paid in those months. The main focus should be on variable costs before moving forward to the fixed expenses.

- **Setting price:** The process of finding your break-even point will facilitate you to set a realistic price based on the total operating expenses of your business.

- **Catch missing expenses:** Since you have to know all expenses before you start figuring out the break-even point, this process of analyzing expenditures helps to identify expenses that otherwise could be caught later or never be identified at all.

- **Set revenue targets:** The process reveals the number of units to be sold before you start making a profit. The figure allows you to plan the number of meals to sell in the given period to reach a projected profit.

- **Make smarter decisions:** The formula allows the management to make decisions based on data and not on personal assumptions or instincts.

- **Limited financial strain:** Since the analysis offers the management the number of plates to be sold to reach certain milestones, this analysis helps to minimize financial surprises down the road.

- **Fund your business:** Before investors offer you their money, normally they always want to know the break-even point. It is one of the very important gauges to access the soundness of any business.

The benefits of the break-even analysis are irreplaceable in many businesses, especially the new ones. You have to make sure you utilize the service of your accountant and come up with this figure before you even start your business. You should understand the number of months or even years where your business will operate under loss. Explore and prepare a solid plan for funding your business in that period to avoid unnecessary disruption of business operations.

## Basic duties of an accountant

Before you start looking for a person who will be dealing with the accounting system of your business, it is better to understand their primary tasks. Generally, the primary duties of the accountant are shown below:

- Prepare tax returns.
- Helps with preparations of starting a business in various aspects when needed.
- Monitor expenditures and revenues.
- Prepare financial statements.
- Prepare financial forecasting and risk analysis reports.
- Prepare accounting ratios for decision-making purposes.
- Acts as an advisor on cost reduction and revenue maximization.
- Ensure the prepared financial statements meet the laws and regulations of the accounting principles.
- Securing financial statements, meanwhile, keeping them up to date.

Accountants can perform additional duties within their accounting guidelines depending on the scope of the contract between the two of you. So do not take for granted all efforts of hiring the right candidate. Play a major role in recruiting process, if you can, to get the right nominee with whom you will be willing to share key information about your business including your business bank accounts. The one who is willing to go the extra mile when your business encounters unforeseeable challenges.

# Functional cash control system

Cash control comprises all procedures put in place to monitor and verify the nature and accuracy of cash received in the business. Moreover, they also screen and authenticate the nature of cash expenditures. Unlike other types of assets, cash and cash equivalents are the most important for the survival of any business. Cash equivalents comprise bank accounts and marketable securities such as shares. Also, it includes other forms of securities with less than 90 days maturity period. Generally, business operations cannot run smoothly without having sufficient cash. If the problem of cash accessibility persists, the chance for the business to collapse is high.

## Benefits of the cash control system

There are plenty of good reasons for having a functional cash control system in your business. Below are some of the advantages you can experience:

- **Reduce operation risk:** When you succeed to install a profound cash control system; automatically, you will reduce or eliminate many cash-related problems such as theft. Which is the number one contributor to premature business failures.

- **Streamlined process:** The functions of all departments of your business will keep moving forward in right the direction when you manage to control the availability of cash. Also, it maximizes the expectations of the internal and external shareholders regarding the survivorship of your business.

- **Eliminate downtime:** Daily business operations process will be guaranteed to operate as scheduled when an ability to finance all basic financial transactions is met.

Collectively, you need to put into place practical procedures of making sure your business is not running out of cash needed to meet daily business operations. Examples of these operations are paying bills, covering the cost of wages and salaries, paying rent, paying vendors, and others. No matter the number of fixed assets you possess in your business, still the power of cash in hand cannot be replaced. It needs your close attention at all times to eliminate the interruption of business operations. Indeed, the presence of operational interruptions will play a direct role to jeopardize the ROI. A situation in which you need to work very hard to minimize or avoid its occurrences completely.

## Financial statement analysis

Financial statement analysis includes the entire process of analyzing the financial statements of your business, mainly to facilitate the decision-making process. You cannot just operate a business without fully understanding the general performance on a periodical basis. Remember, both short and long-term investment decisions should not be performed without first evaluating the stability of your business's finances. Moreover, external shareholders rely mainly on financial statements to understand a wider range of your business performances in addition to the business value. Generally, financial statement analysis includes a balance sheet, income statement, statement of cash flows, and essential supplementary notes.

## Benefits of effective financial statement analysis

Once the financial statements are prepared accurately, they offer numerous valuable benefits to the primary users that are essential to facilitate the smooth operation of the business. Below are just a few of these advantages:

- They provide real-time analysis both to internal and external shareholders. It happens when you generate forecast reports and data models needed to provide well-informed decisions in a timely fashion.
- They also help to evaluate and give the owner detailed indications required to manage debts.
- They allow the decision-makers to monitor business financial performance and compliances as required by law.
- Another important aspect of financial statement analysis is to facilitate basic initiatives of cash flow management.
- They also play a major role to stimulate efficient communication and collaborations between internal and external shareholders.
- When prepared in a timely fashion, they help to expose risk and allow proper remedies to be taken ahead of time before things go bad.
- They also maximize the relationship with business suppliers, one of the key managerial performance tools needed to beat business rivals.

The list of benefits is bigger than indicated above. These essential needs of preparing sound accounting ratios are not to be ignored.

# Managing your finances

The stability of any business starts with having a well-prepared plan and functional discipline in managing finances. No matter the amount of money you have in your account if you failed to put into place significant expenditure arrangements ahead of time; the chance of running out of funds much sooner is high. Having valuable assets alone in your portfolio is not enough to rescue your business from falling if you do not have sufficient cash flow. You need enough cash or cash equivalents to cover all necessary daily business operations to stay afloat.

Take tangible measurements by having a comprehensive business plan that shows projected quarterly, semi-annual, and annual cash needs. Additionally, your financial plan should indicate ways of financing the budget. The budget has to be inclusive with no omission of necessary expenditure transactions. The same applies to your source of income; make sure the mentioned sources are well indicated and reliable to avoid unnecessary disturbances to your business operations. Collective measures of preparing a sound budget should consider the following major points:

- **Pay yourself:** Repeatedly, many small business owners never include their salary in the list of business expenditures. They account for unrealistic profit that does not exist while deducting total expenses from the revenue they made. Strive to avoid this and other similar omissions of necessary transactions in your budget and books of account. If not taken care of, the omission of any transaction brings an unrealistic budget that might undermine or overstate the real situation of your business's financial status. Once allowed to progress for a while, this bad behavior will be one of the major contributors to your failures. Try to utilize the expertise of experienced CPAs to avoid this and related mistakes from not happening.

- **Invest in growth:** Always look ahead of you and try to visualize where your business will be in the next two, three, or five years from now? Put realistic, bold, and attainable goals in a business plan and strive to meet them in real-time. Promptly, correct all discrepancies and learn through mistakes before moving forward victoriously. With the help of existing and advanced technology, build a culture of innovation in your managerial style. Then act accordingly and be ahead of your rivals in many aspects of business operations.

- **Utilize loans when necessary:** Many individuals never like to live with debts. Yes, it is understandable if you plan to take a loan for no apparent reason. When difficult situations happened to your business, sometimes taking a loan is necessary to guarantee the survival of your business. If this situation occurs, make sure you seek only the amount of money you need. Do not take a large amount of a loan just because you have a good credit score and satisfactory collateral that persuade a loan officer to offer you a big amount. Be realistic about your needs and generate efficient ways of paying back in an agreed time frame to avoid paying unnecessary interest and penalties.

- **Maximize business credit:** We all know that in our daily financial lives, there are good times and bad times. The same scenario happens in the business world. When it happens that you need financial help, your efforts of maintaining a good credit history will play a decisive factor in getting the help you need. Satisfactory credit scores also help to secure deals much faster and with reasonable teams in favor of your venture. Good deals are happening a lot in the food industry. Having a good relationship with the bank will help to secure good loans faster. This is a competitive factor against your rivals, utilize it when you can.

- **Satisfactory billing strategy:** Dealing with paying bills in a timely manner is a challenging task for most business owners. Closely, monitor your budget and cash flow statements. Anytime you start experiencing a shortage of cash, develop a practical plan to resolve the problem immediately. All procedures for securing additional funds should be well prepared ahead of time to avoid unnecessary cash flow shortages.

- **Spread out tax payments:** Do not join the club of the majority of small business owners who pay taxes annually. This habit can create a big financial burden on your cash flow and budget. The IRS has set a plan for all business owners to pay taxes quarterly. Try to utilize this option since it allows you to pay a small amount of tax every three months rather than the whole chunk at once. The monthly option also is available. Consider using it if that works better in your business.

- **Monitor your books:** Even though you rely on an accountant to prepare financial books of account, still develop a habit of going through them every few days or weeks. This action will allow you to catch errors in real-time and find proper solutions before becoming severe and damage your operations. Also, it helps to stop stolen money in your bank account either by your accountant or other intruders. When prepared correctly, financial statements offer valuable accounting trends that are more useful in preparing future budgets. And can open the door for developing realistic future forecasts needed to make perceptible decisions at the right time. When you managed to be in line with your decisions, it maintains the valuable stability of your business you need.

- **Focus on both expenditures and ROI:** All major transactions should be allowed after meeting preset internal audit standards. You need to have inclusive standards that explain the purpose of the transaction, justification of the amount needed, the timing of the expenditure, and the impact it brings to the business. Only major transactions that meet all criteria should be allowed to take place, no more.

You need to have a well-structured business that will withstand various mother-nature turbulences and man-made challenges from your rivals. Create state of art procedures and structures for handling and solving these challenges productively and tirelessly. The higher preparations you put in place ahead of time; the better structure will be to prevent and withstand business-related obstacles. The goal is for you to succeed in minimizing occurrences of unnecessary challenges in your business; as well as, knowing how to handle obstacles in a calm manner. Automatically, you will open the door of success necessary to move your business on to meet your vision and beyond.

## Financial ratio analysis

Financial ratio analysis is the method used in the accounting industry to compare the relationship between two or more transactions of the financial data. The process takes place from the financial statements of the business as well as between different companies in the same industry or among industries. To facilitate the comparison process, many options can be utilized, but the most popular one is ratio analysis.

Basically, there are four major groups of the ratios most acceptable accounting boards are using as indicated below:

- **Liquidity ratios**: It comprises the group of ratios that indicate the going concern of the business. They stipulate the operational capability of the business. Examples of the group of liquidity ratios are:
  - The cash coverage ratio
  - The current ratio
  - The quick ratio
  - Liquidity index

- **Activity ratios:** It is a group of ratios that measures the quality and performance of the company managerial team. Examples of activity ratios include:

  - The accounts payable turnover ratio
  - Sales-to-working capital ratio
  - Working capital turnover ratio
  - The accounts receivable turnover ratio
  - Fixed asset turnover ratio

- Inventory turnover ratio

- **Leverage ratios:** They indicate the ability of businesses to utilize debts while financing daily operations. Examples of leverage ratios include:

  - The fixed charge coverage
  - Debt service coverage ratio
  - Debt-to-equity ratio

- **Profitability ratios:** It is a group of ratios that evaluate the ability of the business to generate profit. Generally, examples of profitability ratios include:

  - The margin of safety
  - Return on equity
  - Return on net assets
  - Return on operating assets
  - The contribution margin ratio
  - Gross profit ratio
  - Net profit ratio
  - Break-even point

These and other ratios are so helpful to decision-makers who want to understand all aspects of business operations in real-time. The accuracy of the financial statements is so important to guarantee the chance of getting reliable and useful financial ratios. For this to happen, make sure all business-related transactions are allocated, recorded, and reported to the accountant at a reasonable time to avoid the occurrence of under or over inflations of the financial statements.

Constantly, consult your accountant to ask for these and other important ratios. You need to access the direction of your business before things start falling apart. Request detailed explanations of how to interpret these ratios to avoid missing essential clues needed to make functional and inclusive decisions. Generally, develop a habit of asking questions when you feel you are facing a situation that needs additional clarification. Indeed, this is one of the primary pillars most successful business owners use to sharpen their knowledge. So, do you, right?

## Return on investment (ROI)

Return on investment is defined as a performance measurement used to evaluate the efficiency or profitability of an investment. Moreover, it can also be utilized to compare the efficiency of various investments relative to the total cost spent for each project.

In summary, it reveals the following outcomes:

- It is a profitability metric used to evaluate the performance of each project.
- The formula of ROI can be calculated in percentage format to facilitate the decision process.
- It is so functional to compare projects with the same characteristics while trying to rank them in various formats.
- ROI does not include holding time that might create a challenge of investing money in another project.

Below is a formula to calculate return on investment:

**Return on investment (ROI)**

**ROI = final value – initial value (net return)**

**Return on investment in a percentage format**

**ROI = (final value of investment – initial value of investment / cost of investment) X 100**

**Interpretation of ROI**

- **Positive ROI:** If an investment's ROI is net positive, it is probably worthwhile. But if other opportunities with higher ROIs are available, these signals can help you to eliminate or select the best options to invest in.

- **Negative ROI:** Having a negative result implies a net loss. In the next project, you should strive to avoid any project or investment with a negative ROI, especially when there are more investment opportunities with a positive ROI.

# 9 Basic elements of food cost control

Making a decent profit in your business starts by developing comprehensive measures that will be used to control operating expenses at all levels. You need to identify each segment of your business that can be a source of money leakage. When necessary, consult your accountant, mentor, or any member of your winning club to discuss various measures of minimizing cost in all identified sources of money leakages. Below are some of the areas that need closer attention:

- **Purchasing:** Closely, monitor all purchase transactions and allow only important ones to take place. Utilize all promotions and discounts in the industry to cut down total purchase costs. Consider purchasing cheap alternatives if the quality of the meals will not be compromised.

- **Receiving:** All received products should be documented clearly and in a timely fashion. The date and the name of the person who receive the products must be shown in the documents.

- **Storage:** Proper storage procedures must be prepared ahead of time and be followed by all employees with no exception. All manufacturer storage recommendations must be adhered to by all employees. The same applied to the city codes and the recommendation of the department of health. Remember, you will also cut the cost of food by not allowing unnecessary spoilage to happen.

- **Issuing:** The procedure of issuing the produce out for consumption should be as clear and prepared professionally. When possible, try to document everything that is going out of the store the same way as you do when receiving them. In short, all products leaving the storage room must be traceable in writing to avoid theft.

- **Food preparation:** All food preparation processes should be done in a very considerable manner to avoid throwing away food that should not be considered as waste. Try to minimize the amount of food that goes into the garbage bin, because it is the same as throwing money away carelessly.

- **Portioning:** You need to learn how to portion your plates without making your customers unhappy; and losing money with wasted food. Unless you have set the prices right and customers are allowed to take away any leftovers; otherwise, you might be losing money that you cannot recover.

- **Order taking:** Develop a user-friendly system that can be easy to implement and efficient enough to prevent theft. You must have a clear procedure that indicates all meals leaving the kitchen are to be accompanied by money coming into the counter. The procedure should be effective enough to not allow waiters to save meals for their friends or relatives without pay.

- **Cash receipts:** Do not allow all sever to have access to the cash register. Procedures should be put into place to analyze all safe and appropriate ways of controlling cash until gets deposited into the bank account.

- **Bank deposits/accounts payable:** Closely monitor all transactions going in the business accounts, including the money going out to pay company creditors. Any suspicious transactions must be followed immediately, and proper remedies should be implemented to avoid repetition of the same incidents.

- **Payroll expenses:** Make sure only employees who were on the clock are the ones who get paid. Also, watch closely the number of hours and shifts worked to make sure they are justifiable.

- **Repair expenses:** It does not happen periodically, but when it occurs, it has a chance of seriously effecting your bank account. Most contractors are taking advantage or have the wrong perception that business owners have a lot of money. Also, they are good at fooling those who do not show any knowledge of the problem that needs attention. Try to possess at least an equivocal knowledge of your business areas to avoid this kind of scam.

Always try to be ahead of the game by being so close to events that are happening in your business. Both employees and outsiders never stop taking advantage of the owners who show some sign of incompetence in what is going on in their businesses. Understandably, almost no one possesses all the skills for running a successful business. But do not panic if you fall into this group, the next step to overcome your weakness is to seek professional help. The sooner you secure the help you need, the faster you will stop making costly blunders with your business.

All for-profit business enterprises cannot avoid incorporating sound financial systems into their business culture. Whether you possess an accounting background or not, this is one of the must be done right topics in your business. It has to be evaluated in a detailed manner and put into place immediately after you start your business. Constantly, financial statements must be computed, interpreted, and used in the decision-making process as recommended by your accountant. Liquidity ratios are very important to understand the soundness of your business operations. Because of their importance, it is better to request these ratios every few weeks if not on weekly basis. They will offer you the knowledge needed to direct your business in the right direction. Set aside the timeline of how frequently you need to be supplied with these ratios and communicate with your accountant to establish this operation.

With the help of your accountant, develop a cash plan that shows all sources of the cash and the amount of the cash usage. At the minimum, the two sides must match, or the sources side should be bigger than the consumption counterparts. The goal is to eliminate any chance of running short of cash, a situation that any strong-minded business owner will not want to experience. Periodically, conduct a meticulous evaluation of the functionality and the effectiveness of your cash control system. When you come to any shortcomings, proper remedies should be implemented immediately, including other measures that will not allow the occurrence of the same mistakes again.

# To-Do List Form – Chapter Seven

| Action | Goals | Results(Y/N) |
|---|---|---|
| **Time-sensitive actions:**<br><br>1.<br><br>2.<br><br>3.<br><br>4.<br><br>5.<br><br>6.<br><br>7.<br><br>8.<br><br>9.<br><br>10. | | |
| **Less time-sensitive actions**<br><br>1.<br><br>2.<br><br>3.<br><br>4. | | |

| 5.    |  |  |
|-------|--|--|
| 6.    |  |  |
| 7.    |  |  |
| 8.    |  |  |
| 9.    |  |  |
| 10.   |  |  |

# Read Again Pages – Chapter Seven

| Page # | Topic/Subtopic | Purpose | Result (Y/N) |
|---|---|---|---|
|  |  |  |  |
|  |  |  |  |
|  |  |  |  |
|  |  |  |  |
|  |  |  |  |

# Chapter Eight

## Comprehensive and functional marketing structure

In the business arena, marketing is defined as all activities of promoting the selling of a product or service. It includes supporting activities of advertising, selling, and delivering products to the final users. To raise the level of awareness of your service to the community, various techniques for promoting attention must be implemented. The attention has to be strong enough to persuade them to start coming to eat in your restaurant, order the takeaway, or request the home delivery service. Furthermore, you have to figure out various marketing techniques of persuading customers to keep coming constantly.

## Seven principles of marketing (the 7 Ps)

The process of preparing a sound marketing package is time-consuming. Moreover, most of the time, it requires a substantial amount of money to cover the whole process. Because you need a lot of resources to come up with the right marketing tool, then all essential procedures of preparing it right should be followed to maximize its productivity. For your marketing strategies to be productive, prepare them with considerations of all essential factors among others including:

- **Product:** Clearly, explain the type of food you are selling in your restaurant. The details also should include other related services that you are offering such as wine or catering services.

- **Price:** To avoid getting a lot of phone calls from customers who want to know the price of your services before they decided to come, include these prices in your ads when possible.

- **Promotion:** In a detailed and clear way, explain all promotions you have in your business. The frequency of these promotions also should be stated. When you can, most customers also want to know the available qualifications relating to your marketing campaigns.

- **Place:** The location of your business must be included in your advertisements. Other means of communication such as phone number, email address, or website should be conveyed to the recipients when necessary.

- **People:** Since you have a group of target customers in your business model, all advertisements should be prepared after assessing their primary characteristics, such as their standard of living, educational backgrounds, and purchasing power, among others. The proper balance of all essential characteristics should be made for the message to deliver attention and be more productive.

- **Process:** Promptly, assess all means of delivering your message. Choose only convenient, cheap, and effective ways of reaching your customers.

- **Physical evidence**: Include all essential evidence that demonstrates your physical existence and the functionality of your business. Normally, online customers prefer to see the name, address, and phone number to verify the eligibility of your business versus a fake one.

Anytime you ignore or do not fully pay attention to one or more of these 7 Ps, it means you are opening a door for deficiencies in your marketing campaign. This kind of controllable problem should not be allowed to happen in your business. Generally, competitors are so good to capitalize on mistakes their fellow business owners are making. In a matter of weeks or months, you will find that the damage is so big and costly to comprehend without destabilizing your financial position. The primary question is, why will you allow these and other silly mistakes to keep happening in your business? Remember, most of these are controllable mistakes. Certainly, a smart person like you should not allow them to happen in the first place.

## Creation of an advertisement kit

Depending on your business model, you may invest in advertising your business to meet both the current and the new customers. You must focus first on finding proper means of retaining almost all if not every one of your existing customers. Then you can develop a second plan to seek ways of recruiting the new ones. When you manage to treat your current customers right, they can deliver many benefits to your business such as:
- **Cost-cutting:** It happens through spending less on advertising expenses because it is so cheap to retain current customers compared with the efforts of getting new clientele.

- **More profit:** Generally, loyal customers are more profitable compared with their counterparts. They tend to order a lot of variety of foods regardless of the price. Also, they leave sizeable tips, which play a major role to supplement the wages of the savers.

- **Positive reviews:** They prefer to leave positive reviews, which is one of the free sources of reaching new customers most business owners are struggling to get.

- **Word of mouth:** It is another important action existing customers are so good to deliver to other people. By the way, this is one of the free major pillars I have relaying for the growth of my taxes business.

- **Feedback:** For those business owners who like to get or request feedback, as mentioned, loyal customers are good participants you can rely on.

- **Add new food:** This group of customers also are constantly eager to explore the new food or services you offer. The presence of this kind of enthusiasm helps business owners to reshape their brands including adding new meals.

- **Forgiveness:** Business owners and their team of employees are not immune from making mistakes. When that happens, loyal customers are retaining a high level of forgiveness compared with new customers.

When you succeed to keep almost all of your current customers, it helps to spend less on advertisements. Then any leftover money out of the advertisement budget, you can allocate to recruit new customers. Periodically, assess the effectiveness of the ads and stop them when the target failed to be reached. Alternatively, correct any misalignments before you proceed with the campaigns.

# Advertisement media to choose

The process of advertising your restaurant can be performed in many ways depending on your business model. Below are some of the ways to reach your audiences:

- **Direct calling:** It needs some patience to call a good number of prospective customers daily if you have enough time. You can start by creating a database of the target group. Also, you may outsource the task if you have enough money to pay call centers.

- **Mailing letters:** Try also to locate the list of customers from the phone book. Phone books are distributed annually free of charge. In case you do not have one, you may visit your local library and ask an attendant how to allocate one. Some companies also sell addresses based on the zip codes you want. Most of them operate printing services that they print and mail cards on your behalf. If your budget allows, this route is one of the convenient ways of reaching customers.

- **Dropping ads in the neighborhood:** Try to hire high schoolers who are mostly cheap to perform this task of placing stickers on people's doors. Avoid underpaying them or sending them without proper arrangements. Moreover, assessing other essential factors such as security, weather, distance, and city codes. All these decisive factors must be evaluated very closely before you dispatch them.

- **Buy TV air time:** Once created inclusively and aired in prime time, TV ads are the most persuasive media with the ability to reach many people. However, most small restaurateurs do not have sufficient capital to cover the budget for TV ads. If your budget allows for you to jump on this wagon, the expected rewards are much more promising compared with most public awareness media. For the rewards of TV ads to be fruitful to your business; thoughtfully, evaluate the projected expenditures and the outcomes ahead of time before making or buying airtime from your local TV station. As always, locate research data that justify a particular cost to be spent and the number of leads it creates. In case the data works on your side for indicating more leads that cover all the ad expenditures and bring a promising profit to your business, then you can decide to undertake that route. The opposite is true, do not burn your money if you do not possess supporting statistics to back up your action.

- **Make a radio ad:** Placing an ad on your local radio stations is another useful way of spreading your message to your prospective customers. It is less expensive than purchasing a TV ad, but still, it is far more expensive than other means of disseminating the message to your target groups. Try to exercise due diligence when making this fruitful but daring money spending decision.

- **Enlist online platforms:** The presence of many ways of advertising or listing businesses online helps many technology-savvy business owners to stay afloat in the business arena under a limited budget. Some of these websites such as Craigslist, Next Door, Garage Sale, and Metta marketplace, among others are free of charge and are worth utilizing to your advantage. Once you experience various online techniques of maneuvering around jargon and obstacles; the road is wide enough to propel your business ahead of your competitors.

- **Buy space in local printouts:** There is a good number of ads circulating magazines, bulleting, and others that open a door for business owners. They are less expensive compared to placing an ad on TV or radio stations. However, any money spent on these ads should be monitored making sure they produce tangible outcomes.

- **Drop business cards or brochures in hot spot areas:** A well-prepared business person carries business cards anywhere he/she goes. I hope you will be one of them who is capable of spotting all potential areas and leave your business card to spread the message of your business free of charge. You can drop your business cards in laundry places if they allow doing that or other small business places that are willing to help their local small business owners to advertise their ventures. Your CPA office is another hot spot to allocate some new leads. Ask your accountant if they have a table or a corner spot for holding business cards including outsiders like you.

- **Maximize networking gear:** The creation of networking links with various sources can be done in many forms including engaging in volunteering activities in your local area. When you make your name and your business be known in the place you live, it helps to open more potential leads much easier. The idea is to let your neighbors know what you are doing, which might help to build a big trust in your business.

Again, having comprehensive preparations of how to advertise your business will save you a lot of time and money; meanwhile, maximizing the outcomes of your efforts. Doing nothing is not a strategy whatsoever. Do not let your business riva.ls run effective marathon ads ahead of yours. Combine both freeways of reaching your customers together with other media that you have to spend some money on. According to Gourmet Marketing, the average budget for marketing expenses in the restaurant industry is 3 to 6 percent of the total revenue. For example, if your business made a total sales of $600,000 in the first quarter of 2022, then the budget for advertising in the second quarter of 2022 should be between $18,000 and $36,000.

## Having well-designed signage

Like a business card, the signage carries the image of your business on a large scale. With no excuses, your business signage should be appealing to withstand the competition from your opponents. Consider the following factors while designing your signage:

- **Color:** Choose the right combination of colors, which will possess high persuasive power.

- **Design and graphics:** Any graphics that are going together with your signage should be well designed to maximize its look. Also, to deliver the intended message right away when someone sees it.

- **Font and size:** The font size of the words should be taken very seriously with consideration of the distance from the nearby roads and the height from the ground.

- **Lighting:** Inside lights play a major role, especially at night time. If the city zone allows for the installation of animations, consider utilizing that opportunity.

- **Materials:** Consider choosing high-quality materials that will withstand the local weather and test of time.

Check with your landlord before you spend a lot of money creating beautiful signage that might not be allowed on the business premise. The same situation might happen with the city zoning codes. Some cities are more restricting than others. To be on the safe side, consult your local city office and get their opinion on what can be done to stay on the safe side of the equation.

## Factors to consider in determining an advertising budget

In the business field, you are not advised to spend money unwisely just because you expect more money down the road. All transactions must be justifiable including the timing of expenditure. The same philosophy should be followed in the advertisement budget. Try to develop attainable procedures while preparing your ads and the accountability measures that will track the execution process. To attain this goal, utilize many factors including:

- **Projected ROI:** You have to come up with a comprehensive plan explaining in detail the primary and secondary goals you want to achieve. Make sure these goals are realistic and attainable in the allocated time frame.

- **Select target recipients:** The degree of effectiveness of the ads will be reached when you know the customers you want to target. You have to understand their basic characteristics that determine the way they make decisions.

- **Type of foods, service, or promotion:** Specify your ad on a particular nature of the product or products you want to raise the level of awareness. It includes all types of food you sell or just a few of them. Also, the focus might be directed on the new kinds of foods, services, or promotions. Some ads can also be prepared just to enforce the preview ads. The general message is to make sure you target the right type of foods, services, or promotions with the right message, price, and coverage.

- **Media selection:** As stated above, there are numerous types of media to be used while disseminating your message to the recipients. Some are free, others are a little bit cheap, and the last group comprises of expensive media such as TV. Remember, price alone should not be a conclusive aspect. Consider other kinds of factors such as total coverage area, speed of delivery, and persuasive power before you make the final decision.

- **Projected profit:** You must set ahead of time the projected earnings you want to achieve. While preparing this goal, try not to under or over-inflate the figure to avoid being disappointed when you failed to reach the goals when you set them too high. Also, when the goals are so low, you might slow down the campaign. It happens when you start thinking you are doing an awesome job, without knowing that you are lagging behind your competitors.

- **Ad duration:** Along with other factors, make sure you set a time limit for transmitting your advertisements. The benefit of doing this is to get enough time to assess the effectiveness of your campaign. If you are experiencing positive results, you can consider placing new ads, again for a given period.

- **Operational cost:** Try to stay within budget at all times, to avoid unnecessary interruption of other essential services. For instance, when you take off the payroll money to cover the ads costs; you might open a chain of problems that are costly and difficult to stop. Assume you do not have enough money to cover wages; in this scenario, expect some if not all employees to stop coming to work. From there, a lot of additional problems will start to erupt.

- **Long-term goals:** In the end, the goals of each ad must collaborate with the long-term goals of the entire business. They have to be prepared with an intention of achieving the collective business long-span milestones.

These assessments are so beneficial in deciding what to be done next. If the goal is met, then you can decide whether to stop or set another major milestone. In case the outcomes were disappointing, do not ground the campaign without first evaluating what went wrong. When you notice a correctable problem then you can fix it and try another round. If you did not notice any problems, the quick conclusion might be the ad itself is not working. Then find another route of bringing a better and more productive ad to replace the old one.

## Factors that limit the performance of the ads

Generally, many contributing factors might play a part in reducing the performance of the ad outcomes. Some of the factors are:

- **Less time:** It happens when you want your goals to be attained in a very short time beyond the industrial average. Constantly, strive not to fall into this trap many inexperienced business owners do.

- **Wrong media:** When you decided to send your ads using unpopular or unfamiliar media to the audiences, the results might be lower than the expectations. Assume you want to air an ad on your local TV station; yet most of your target customers do not have a cable or own TV. For example, the percentage of those who have access to TV is only 25 percent. Out of this small number, 50 percent have a complicated schedule that barely gets even 10 minutes a day to watch TV. In this scenario, there is no way your ad will be effective.

- **Poor schedule:** If you choose to air your ad in the morning because it is cheap compared with the evening time. Then you have to understand that the number of viewers is low to justify the price. The opposite is true when placing the ad in prime time where the number of viewers is high, and you have to pay more.

The season is another factor to take into account to maximize the results of your ads. Consider the same example above, let's say you place an ad in prime time - after working hours. However, it happens to be in January that is accompanied by a lot of snow and freezing rain. In this situation, even though the ad is in prime time, the weather will play a major role in preventing your customers showing up to your restaurant. In the end, the effectiveness of your ad might produce mixed-signal results.

- **Wrong customers:** The efforts of advertising your business to the wrong customers will just be a waste of money. For instance, always expect low turnover when you try to convince Mexicans to eat Italian dishes.

- **Poor research:** Relaying your message or group of customers from unrealistic data is another poor managerial decision to make. Save money by seeking correct and inclusive data. Not running ads this way will be deadly to your business.

- **Wrong message:** Make sure you cross-check the message to ensure it is the one that is intended to be delivered. The message can be wrong for instance, then you keep advertising while the promotion no longer exists.

- **Unrealistic claims:** Avoid spreading the message that cannot be supported by reality. Any type of message that is misleading your customers can discourage customers from not coming to buy your food again. Moreover, it might trigger a lawsuit that might be costly for your business to afford.

  For instance, when you claim that all of your meals are made from organic ingredients. The moment the customers realize that is not true, let me say this, you will have to close your business. The power of social media alone is so strong, no matter your title or the position of your parents or relatives. Try to be very careful to avoid your wonderful long-term goals, visions, and dreams being cut off prematurely.

Avoid unrealistic determinations from each ad you convey to your customers. All essential measures of preparing inclusive and effective ads are to be followed with no excuse. These measures are essential to get the results you deserve. Also, you want to enjoy the time you are investing in your business milestones. Failure to perform your assignment will create tension in your business cash flow. A situation that you must avoid at all costs. It is so common for the problems to flow down to the employees that might trigger some of them to start looking for jobs somewhere else.

## Design tips that will attract more customers

Various techniques should be explored, evaluated, and utilized to maximize the revenue of your business. Constantly, apply the contents of the winning equation while figuring out new strategies for persuading customers to keep coming. You should set up first the efficient ways of maximizing the retention rate before you start recruiting new customers. Generally, the cost of keeping a current customer is much cheap compared with the efforts of convincing new people to be regular customers. Below are some of the techniques you may apply to reach this target sooner:

- **Invest in concept, style, and theme:** Put your design knowledge into practice to make your restaurant look more attractive than your competitors. If you do not have enough knowledge in this field, consider hiring someone who has enough experience and who understands your vision and long-term goals. Both the interior and exterior of your business should be given close attention.

- **Eye-catching entrance:** The entrance is a starting point for explaining your business. Make sure the entire exterior area also complements the look of the main entrance. Its design should consider your customers and a little bit beyond their imaginations too.

- **Choose color combinations wisely:** Do not take for granted the beauty of the right color combinations. Make sure all efforts of testing color applications have been exhausted. The goal is to maximize the look of your restaurant to current and new customers will be looking forward to coming in.

- **Design and layout:** Everything that is going inside of your business should:

  - Have a major purpose of being there.
  - An ability to complement other pieces.
  - To be placed in the right position, among others.

Do not let the dining area look like a display gallery, there is no need to do that. Let the natural look and the business model lead you when designing these important areas of your business.

- **Invest in nice HVAC**: During the summertime; especially, on scotch heat days, do not expect to get enough customers if your air conditioner is not working perfectly. Even those few customers you will get, most of them will not feel comfortable ordering extra meals when the dining room is so hot. Make sure you make a proper plan for this crucial investment in your business to have a pleasant place for your customers to enjoy while eating their meals.

- **Utilize the advantage lights:** You cannot ignore the power of lights in adding beauty of your restaurant. When selected and set properly, lights will be one of the significant magnets for attracting more customers. If your knowledge is running short in the field, do not hesitate to seek external help from professionals.

- **Find an irresistible aroma:** This is one of the trickier projects to undertake. Getting a natural and appealing aroma to suit almost all customers is hard. However, when you succeed, the benefits are significantly huge in attracting more customers.

- **Music:** Who can resist the power of music in changing the mood? Now the task is, how can you choose nice music to conquer the minds of your customers? When you managed to get it right, the outcomes are apparent.

- **Understand your customer's needs:** That is why I said early you have to start by selecting the target market before developing a business model. Once you know the group of the market to target, then you can explore the food-related problems your restaurant will going to solve. The next step is to develop an appealing menu to meet the desires of your customers.

- **Maximize the outdoor outlook:** Exterior side of the building should not be ignored. New customers will not even bother to stop in your place if it is not spotless. The problem can be even worse when they can find a clean and nicer restaurant near yours selling identical food.

Start by looking at your competitors' buildings, then renovate yours to be much nicer. If your budget allows, you can bring new and irresistible design ideas that your competitors cannot afford or have a hard time imitating.

- **Craft a pleasant bathroom:** This is one of the essential projects in the restaurant business that must be done with no cutting corners. No matter how attractive the dining room is, the mistake of having a dirty and outdated bathroom will put off the majority of your customers. It will leave a lasting memory.

- **Eliminate problem areas:** Be ahead of the game by correcting any issues soon after they happen. For instance, when you notice a leaking roof, you have to fix it right away rather than waiting for the water to drip on the head of the customer. In the business world, we call this action of waiting for the customers to complain "the damage is done".

The business that you have been dreaming of for so long will not start growing fast as you have envisioned without investing in the marketing field. Customers need to be aware of what you are selling before they can start coming. Moreover, the efforts to keep persuading them must be implemented in the effort of maximizing the retention rate. From there, you can move to the next step by looking at new customers and how to convince them to abandon your competitors and join your efforts.

The ads you will use to reach your customers should be prepared using well-researched data. Also, the person who designs, prepares, and submits them should possess enough experience in this field. You want to avoid unnecessary mistakes that will cost your business a lot of time and money, without forgetting tension within the company. Like any other type of transaction in your business, these ads must be organized within the preset boundaries that meet the culture and business model. These boundaries also must be extended including other factors like the financial position of your company and the short and long-term business goals.

In the end, you want to experience positive outcomes that will meet the financial goals of your business. Also, the results must possess satisfactory elements to satisfy the needs of both internal and external shareholders. When all these parts are managed, your long-standing objectives will have a higher chance of being attained in real-time. This is true also for the business ROI.

# To-Do List Form – Chapter Eight

| Action | Goals | Results(Y/N) |
|---|---|---|
| Time-sensitive actions:<br><br>1.<br><br>2.<br><br>3.<br><br>4.<br><br>5.<br><br>6.<br><br>7.<br><br>8.<br><br>9.<br><br>10. | | |
| Less time-sensitive actions<br><br>1.<br><br>2.<br><br>3.<br><br>4. | | |

| | | |
|---|---|---|
| 5. | | |
| 6. | | |
| 7. | | |
| 8. | | |
| 9. | | |
| 10. | | |

# Read Again Pages – Chapter Eight

| Page # | Topic/Subtopic | Purpose | Result (Y/N) |
|---|---|---|---|
|  |  |  |  |
|  |  |  |  |
|  |  |  |  |
|  |  |  |  |
|  |  |  |  |

# Chapter Nine

*"The true entrepreneur is a doer and not a dreamer!"*

*Nolan Bushnell*

## Techniques of growing a successful restaurant business

Welcome to the business world!

Please, allow me to call you a business owner/partner. Okay, you are not there yet? How about "prospect business owner"? Are we on the same page now? I think the answer is yes, thank you.

Now, you are as so close to starting your own restaurant and becoming a chief operating officer (CEO). The one who carries all the daily business operations and has a chance of enjoying the advantages of independence existing in this business arena. As you are heading in this remarkable direction, I will keep walking with you through the remaining essential steps for reaching there much sooner and in a prolific manner.

Moreover, the discussion will allow you to start your business with as many minimal challenges as possible. All this is happening in an attempt of maximizing every single minute of your time invested in this business in addition to getting the satisfactory profit you deserve.

## Educate yourself in the managerial field

Managing daily business operations requires possession of many skills. It depends on the nature and structure of the business; some skills might be more important in one type of business or industry compare to another. For instance, the skills like hiring the right employees, how to delegate power, among others, could play a major role in your managerial practice, compared with someone with no employees at all. The list of management skills you and your managers should possess is as follow:

- **Analytical thinking:** You have to develop the skills needed to identify and define problems. As a CEO of your company, you must comprehend the ability to explore data and get the essential information you need to develop useful solutions to resolve challenges in your business.

- **People management:** Unfortunately, being a business owner means you are wearing the crown of managing others. For this concept to produce satisfactory results, you must be able to put together your workers and team members such as millionaire club members, accountants, and loan managers to share the common goal of running a successful business.

- **Business knowledge:** This is the knowledge that can easily be obtained through devoting ample time to learning. You can get education through reading books, attending seminars, passing-on information from your team members, among others.

- **Leadership:** It comprises all skills of setting and achieving functional and attainable goals. The efforts to fulfill both the short and long-term goals of your business will be reached much easy when you equip yourself with this valuable skill.

- **Budgeting and finance:** As a business owner you also possess a primary duty of being a good guide of your finances. You have to be so good at knowing all incoming and outgoing funds, including the timing of each transaction. In the end, your businesses cash flow will stay positive and strong to finance daily business operations with fewer hiccups.

- **Communication:** This is one of the most important skills in your daily business operations. Consider the following five tips:

  - Use the right channel for conveying your messages.
  - With no excuse, consider who your audiences are.
  - Try to use short and clear words or sentences. Avoid jargon.
  - Be ready to provide answers to almost all questions that are coming to you.
  - According to Professor Mehrabian, in the normal course of running a business, almost 93 percent of communication is nonverbal. So, you must understand productive methods of dealing with nonverbal ways of communicating.

- **Hiring:** Definitely, the hiring task will be up to you. All the time, develop workable ways of handling this mission in a less stressful manner. Meanwhile, being able to allocate the right employees who are ready to generate positive ROI in a satisfactory period.

- **Collaboration and Teamwork:** The restaurant business deals with a bunch of human beings working together to achieve a target milestone. You will just be one element in a group of many. To stay focused and productive, you have to learn various techniques for making all members within the group feel inclusive and valued in the due course of their duties with you.

- **Time Management:** That is why they say, "time is money". I highly agree with this statement. In the real world, you will have a hard time succeeding in life if you never value the importance of time management. In the business arena, it is even worse. You have to make sure you utilize every minute of your time in a productive way, no excuse. Otherwise, you might find yourself following the wagon without knowing where it is going. That is sad…

- **Conflict resolution:** Once you are in a business that deals with a lot of people, it is just a matter of time, misunderstandings will occur. That is just one side of the coin, another one is how are you going to be resolving problems in a win-win fashion. This is a skill that can be acquired through learning.

- **Office management:** Since you will be running the managerial duties, you must quickly learn all duties of running an office, and much more. You have to know how to pay bills on time, arrange documents, take care of guests, clean your office, and much more.

- **Logistics:** Products always need to be moved from stores to your restaurant. Even though you may decide to let some vendors deliver them to your business doorstep; however, not all the products you need will be delivered this way. So, you have to purchase from your local stores. Then get prepared to come up will a plan B for dealing with transportation issues when the primary plan fails.

- **Delegation:** Surely, the delegation concept is so applicable in the restaurant industry. All the time you will be dealing with many workers on each shift. The chance of being around all the time is impractical. To resolve this issue, you have to hire managers who will be running the business when you are not around. This kind of delegating the work needs experience for both sides to stay on one page. The skill that you must possess before you start your business.

- **Negotiating**: When you manage to possess high negotiation skills, with no time, you realize the importance of it as you run your business. For example, you can utilize the skill of accepting quotes from a third party. You have to know the right time to open a discussion to get better deals for your business. When it is appropriate, stop accepting anything coming to your table, engage in productive negotiations first. That is the way successful business owners run their businesses.

- **Planning:** No planning skills at your fingertips, not business. Bottom line. So, do not allow this challenge to consume your fortune.

The list is indeed long to draw some level of pressure on ordinary people. You might be asking yourself, how I can be capable of holding all those skills at once. However, you do not require to possess all of them to run a successful business. Utilize the advantages of the power of the delegation technique to relieve the heavy burden from your shoulders. Moreover, the presence of various club team members also helps to inject essential missing skills in real-time.

# The additional important factor to work on

**Working on your strengths and weaknesses:** It is a better idea to go through your list of strengths, which act as the strong section of advantages you bring into the business. At the same time, it works better once you identify areas that are dragging you down when it comes to the process of running a successful business. For example, if you are not good at accounting, you better accept that deficit and find someone else to cover that important position. Make sure all essential weaknesses have been identified and comprehensive measures have been put in place to overcome them. Failure to find appropriate solutions at the right time, your business operations will struggle to meet target goals.

**Be organized:** Unfortunately, you cannot run away from this crucial habit. The restaurant business involves a lot of sub-projects; sometimes, that have to be run together. Expect to be dealing with so many crews in your business at once. In addition to employees, you will be working with vendors and independent contractors who will be depending on you to give details of what needs to be done. You need to have a high level of respectable composure, a sense of the human, and an adequate systemizing habit. All these are primary ingredients to help you to meet a reasonable level of running daily business operations productively.

**Keep detailed records:** Even though you might have an accountant to handle all accounting activities, still you have a primary duty of collecting and handling all receipts and other essential accounting documents to your CPA. If you decide to handle this yourself, then you also have to pay attention to what type of information you have, where are they located, and how long you have to retain them. The duration of holding the documents has to satisfy all major beneficiaries besides yourself such as the IRS, financial institutions, state and local government, among others.

**Strive to handle risks very well:** The same as our regular lives, running a business always is accompanied by a high level of risk that requires your full attention before things start falling apart. As the business grows, so do the number of threats start growing. To overcome this and other related factors, you need to have detailed risk management plans in place. The plan should have a list of all possible threats in your industry. Then prepare a wide range and functional solutions for each threat. Likewise, try to come up with articulated execution procedures that are less expensive, easy to execute, and with less damage to the business and society in general.

**Be consistent:** This type of habit is so productive in this industry. To save time and money, it is a good idea to start by experimenting with your business ideas. Assume you want to be very consistent with the way you cook and save your meals. You can start let's say by choosing the most popular dishes with your customers. Then move to the next stage of developing the cooking instructions and decent ways of serving the meal to the customers. Once you are pleased with the entire process, then those can be the standards for each meal you cook. In other words, develop a cooking instructions book/pamphlets that are simple for everyone to understand. But they have to be detailed enough to deliver all essential instructions.

The benefits of being consistent with the service you deliver to your customers are shown below:

- It allows you to establish a high degree of awareness in your business operations.
- It facilitates building trust and delivering your services efficiently and profitably.
- Maintaining an adequate consistent culture in your business, which helps to deliver better customer service.
- It maximizes greater customer satisfaction.
- It elevates confidence in attaining business stability.

**Maximize customer service:** Being a CEO of your business requires you to adopt a reasonable level of dealing with people around you. Examples of individuals you will encounter in this business are customers, employees, vendors, club members, and contractors, among others. Assume, intentionally or accidentally you exchange bad words with one of your vendors. In the next few days you might forget what you have told him. However, data shows that most people, for a long period, never forget what someone made them feel bad about. Applying sufficient behavior of treating your team members well. It helps to elevate satisfaction among employees and external shareholders. In turn, the productivity in your business will start going up.

**Take advantage of technology:** Advancements in technology have revolutionized the way business operates. When utilized properly, the technology has a good number of benefits to the restaurant industry as shown below:

- **Ease of access to information:** With help of the computer, tablets, or smartphones; use them accordingly to benefit your business. One of the primary advantages of these devices is the ability to access information anywhere you are, at any time, and in many ways.

- **It saves time:** The time used to go to the library to search for information is considered as old fashion by most people. If you want to allocate the new vendor, just open your smartphone, and there you are, the choices are at your fingertips. The online searching process can be done anywhere regardless of the time and the day of the week. As a business owner, this is an awesome opportunity that needs to be utilized effectively if you want to stay ahead of your competitors.

- **Easy mobility:** Moving from one location to another is much easy and can be done much faster due to the advanced automotive industry. The presence of car rentals such as Uber, Lift, and others have paved the way for dealing with a transportation issue, which is one of the major problems for the new owners with limited starting capital.

- **Cost efficiency:** The availability of affordable means of communication has benefited the restaurant business in cost management. A lot of activities can be computerized to speed up production and minimize operating expenses. For instance, the majority of vendors allow the orders to be done online, inventory management to be computerized, also the accounting system, among others.

When done properly, the technology facilitates to minimize the operating cost of payroll, human error, theft, time-consuming, and so on.

**Be ready to fail and learn from mistakes:** As a newcomer in this industry, you will be facing many challenges that force you to make mistakes. Although mistakes are not good for the business but can be minimized or eliminated when you build a state of art culture of learning new things as quickly as possible. Try to utilize the knowledge of club members in your circle to the fullest. If you have a mentor, give him/her a chance to teach you things that you are not comfortable doing alone. Ask questions when necessary, rather than allowing your shy behavior or ego to overpower your actions.

At the same time, create a habit of not allowing past mistakes to keep happening over and over again. Mistakes are a killer to your business operations. Allow only unavoidable ones to penetrate your daily business operations, while looking for permeant solutions to eradicate them. Use those challenges to your advantage by asking yourself why they are happening, what functional actions should be done to overcome them, and lastly what are takeaway lessons to learn from those mistakes.

## Availability of the reliable transport

Unless you have reliable transport in place, then you do need to worry about this issue. The restaurant business involves a lot of movements of items. As a new business owner, you have to figure out how this process of delivering items to your building in a very effective manner. Many options should be put on the table to facilitate a selection process. Try to identify the pros and cons of each one before concluding what the best choice will be preferable to save your needs. When possible, try to involve your mentor in discussing the better route to undertake to avoid unnecessary delays in getting suppliers. Also, you want to avoid paying a lot of money for something that can be handled differently based on the available resource around your area. Below are options you can consider while figuring out transportation concerns to your business:

- **Purchase own car:** I have seen some restaurateurs start their business by purchasing a pickup or van ahead of time. If it is a good idea to take this route, then go for it. However, I do not recommend starting your business this way unless you have enough capital. Also, you have sufficient knowledge that guarantees you the possibility of breaking-even shortly before you start running out of cash. Another point to consider is to make sure you can utilize the car to maximum to meet the purpose of purchasing it.

- **Using rentals:** Alternatively, you can consider starting your business by using a rental pickup or van in handling your transportation needs. It might not be a good idea in the long run; however, it works well in the short run. At the same time try to utilize your trifling working capital in building your business.

The main advantage of renting the truck only when needed is that it saves a lot of money. You do not have to worry about a van or truck sitting idle and not being used effectively. In addition, it is a waste of money to possess a truck that you do not need when your business is small. Furthermore, the option also takes away the burden of holding and protecting the truck twenty-four seven while it is in your possession. If anything goes wrong with the truck, you will be responsible for repairing any damage or loss.

Your business structure determines whether it allows all items you need in your business to be delivered by someone. Otherwise, you have to set a plan to resolve this important issue. Some new business owners have either a car, van, or pickup capable of transportation services. Others do not have any. If you do not possess any mode of transportation or it is unreliable, then consider buying or renting a car. Either way, try not to go beyond your budget and the daily usability of the vehicle.

## Security/risk; consideration

The entire aspect of dealing with business-related security issues is to unfold various essential scenarios that might play a big role to protect your venture from various kinds of risk. You must have a solid plan ahead of time of how your business and its investments will be protected from all types of destruction such as fire, theft, burglary, and scam, among others. The last thing any business owner wants to see is occurrences of unexpected events that destruct smooth operations of the business or loss of income. Some of these issues might even be bad for your business to the point of starting to take away a portion of your working capital without your knowledge, ability to control, or to stop them.

No one wants to start a business with the motive of losing money. For this concept to materialize, you need to sit down and go through a security plan before you open your business. You need broad measures in place that will guide you in executing necessary actions of preventing destructors from happening in your business. If that fails, then you want to be in a position of handling these destructors in an orderly fashion. In a way that your daily business operations should not be affected. You must utilize your crisis management plan to slow down any form of destruction to the lowest level possible.

Any business whether it is for-profit or not must have a well-prepared *crisis management plan* that is reviewed and amended periodically. Because of this fact, your business is not immune from not having this plan. All key departments of your business must be involved in the preparation process of this plan. Make sure it is detailed enough and inclusive of all matters concerning your business operations. It has to analyze in totality what to be done to prevent unexpected problems from not happening. In case Mother Nature allows these events to happen anyway, then it has to state clearly what functional steps are to be followed to mitigate the problem with minimal damage possible. Also, it should indicate personnel that will be responsible to perform all types of actions and in which order to avoid causing unnecessary confusion or time wastage. In addition, all employees in your business should be educated or attend drills to practice the procedures ahead of time before the accuracy of the actual incident. For reference purposes, the crisis management manual should be kept in a safe place but accessible to all key essential participants when needed.

Below is the list of the essential actions to be taken to ligate the occurrence of calamities in your business:

**Insurance:** Make sure your business possesses all types of essential insurance to protect against various forms of accidents. With no excuse or delay, the building must be insured before you take over the possession rights of the property. Start requesting quotes ahead of time and after agreeing with the insurance company on the type of coverage you prefer to purchase, go ahead and pay the down payment. Sign all essential documents to validate its existence in advance. What you need to notify the insurance personnel is the date of signing the contract for the property. Sometimes, most of the communications with the insurance personnel are done over the phone. However, try to avoid offering inaccurate information to lower the value of the property, which in return, will lower your monthly payment.

When the accident occurs, you want to have enough compensation to cover all damages without forcing you to dig into your pocket to cover the difference. Be as honest as possible and if you do not know anything about a particular question, just admit that you do not have an answer at that time of the interview and you are willing to research the needed information at the earliest possible opportunity.

Make sure all employees who are working on your property are insured. There are four types of insurance an employer can decide to insure their workers.

- **Workers' compensation:** This is a type of insurance that all employers are required to have when they hire employees. It slightly differs from one state to another. Generally, it helps to pay on behalf of the worker's employer to recover from work-related injury or illness. It acts as temporary disability benefits. Moreover, receiving this compensation, allows employees to sign a waiver of the right to sue the employer.

- **Disability insurance:** It is a type of insurance that covers workers when they get injured and be unable to work. Check with your local states about the mandate of offering this insurance. So far, five states have state-mandated employers to carry disability insurance, namely: California, Hawaii, New Jersey, New York, and Rhode Island. Puerto Rico also has this law active for its employers.

- **Health insurance:** No law requires small employers to carry health insurance to their employees. However, when your business starts to grow up, the mandates carried by the Adorable Care Act (ACA) will start to kick in.

- **Life insurance:** This is 100 percent optional whether you want to ensure your workers or not. You are not obligated by law to do that.

For the independent contractors, it is their duty to make sure all of their employees have full coverage. You can use common sense to discuss this point when entering into a contract with someone. For big companies like vendors, you do not need to worry much. There are a lot of watchdogs monitoring their daily business operations on your behalf.

**Lights:** Maximize security on your premises by installing sufficient lighting in essential areas surrounding your building. Make sure available light fixtures are operating properly, without forgetting to replace burnout bulbs. Even though you might find bulbs are working, I always make sure all bulbs surrounding my properties are LED. These are energy-efficient bulbs that help cut down the consumption of electricity.

Research data showed that improved exterior lighting could be an effective crime prevention tool. It improves surveillance and increases the chance of detecting offenders. People feel safer in well-illuminated areas because it has the potential to deter crime.

Most of the time, the cost of the light bulbs is less expensive than dealing with burglary. The damage thieves will leave on your property or customers' properties, such as a broken door or window, cost a lot of money to fix. Moreover, thieves might also take a lot of valuable items that will cost you thousands and your customers a lot of money to replace them. Be realistic when accessing the rate of crime in the location of your property and utilize the data by taking the necessary actions promptly.

**Fire extinguisher unity**: Make sure you install enough fire extinguishers in your business. Employees have to be trained and understand all sources of fire occurrences while trying to find possible ways of preventing them. Make sure all your crews know where to locate fire cylinders when needed. Moreover, everyone on the site has to know how to use them. Gradually, check the expirations dates and replace the expired cylinders with the new ones right away.

**Security system**: Installing a security system in your business is a good option. However, the risk increases if the property is located in a high crime location, which is not worth ignoring. The more valuable your business is, the higher the chances are of getting severe material damage when crime happens. It is a good idea to put a solid plan in place ahead of time so that employees understand how safety procedures will be executed. Most companies are charging reasonable prices most business owners can afford. Shop around to get a good deal based on the needs of your business.

Try to stay abreast of any issues that have a high chance of occurring in your business. More importantly, prepare yourself for all or almost all disasters, even those that play a major role in adding damage to your business operations. The last thing you want to experience in business is seeing challenges that slow down business operations. You do not want to uncover obstacles that bring losses to your venture and completely derail the entire operations to a standstill. Lack of comprehensive preparations is one of the major factors that force most businesses to close their operations for good. Why risk failure after failure when you have a chance to educate yourself ahead of time. Instantly apply the knowledge you received from this book in all areas of your business operations. Try to protect the capital you earned by shielding your business from any form of calamities.

# To-Do List Form – Chapter Nine

| Action | Goals | Results(Y/N) |
|---|---|---|
| **Time-sensitive actions:**<br><br>1.<br><br>2.<br><br>3.<br><br>4.<br><br>5.<br><br>6.<br><br>7.<br><br>8.<br><br>9.<br><br>10. | | |
| **Less time-sensitive actions**<br><br>1.<br><br>2.<br><br>3.<br><br>4. | | |

| | | |
|---|---|---|
| 5. | | |
| 6. | | |
| 7. | | |
| 8. | | |
| 9. | | |
| 10. | | |

# Read Again Pages – Chapter Nine

| Page # | Topic/Subtopic | Purpose | Result (Y/N) |
|--------|----------------|---------|--------------|
|        |                |         |              |
|        |                |         |              |
|        |                |         |              |
|        |                |         |              |
|        |                |         |              |

# Conclusion

Thank you for being together on our journey of enlightening you on this major and bold decision of becoming a business owner. The idea of opening a restaurant business in your area is an essential milestone to undertake while preparing to declare financial freedom in your life. Doing nothing is not a strategy. HOPE is not a strategy either.

Statistics have shown that the industry has started to revamp again after being affected by the aftermath of the covid-19. People have secured their freedom of movement and the ability to keep enjoying life as they used to do before the pandemic. In the business world, this moment is called *opportunity*. More than ever, this is the right moment to start your restaurant business while people are ready to spend their savings to lower the stress of being locked down for almost two years. Do not let the opportunity which is within your grasp pass away without grabbing it.

This book has explained a lot of topics that are essential while preparing to join this industry. You have learned the importance of choosing the right type of food to serve for your target customers. In return, the concept of knowing your customers ahead of time will also help to select the right type of restaurant to start. The one with an opportunity to make a lot of money in a short period.

The need to open a millionaire club has been demonstrated in a detailed manner to facilitate all efforts of fulfilling your visions much sooner. Now you know the importance of this club and how to start recruiting the members. The procedures for retaining and running the club also have been delivered to you in a detailed fashion for your benefit. So, start calling your friends, relatives, co-workers, and others right away in an attempt of putting your money-making ideas into practice.

The knowledge of building a strong and productive foundation for your business was discussed in chapter three. Now you have a winning equation that comprises profound logic, tremendous creativity, and critical thinking. In each stage of your business formation, make sure you effectively utilized this question in all of the decisions you make to get better, stronger, and more dynamic outcomes. Do not take for granted the power of how, why, and when. Before you take an action, you have to ask yourself key questions about the importance and the timing, including the projected outcomes of your activities. Only those with justifiable reasons should prevail.

Do not start your business without first preparing a comprehensive and functional business plan. This is the road map that you cannot run away from, uncles you want to burn your capital with no tangible outcomes to it. Make sure you start the right business formation, whether that be sole appropriate ship, partnership or corporation. Consult your lawyer if you do not possess enough knowledge to understand the best option to choose.

The knowledge you get to pick the right customers to save, the productive location for your business, and the right employees to work with you, should not be taken lightly. These and other key decisions are important points to consider and to be executed well to maximize the return on investment of your business.

Pay attention to where you will be getting your supplies, including setting the state of art procedures for storing them without minimizing their quality. Install well-designed inventory control procedures that are simple but easy to execute and be able to produce the projected outcomes such as cutting down on food spoilage and control of theft.

In case you get time to educate yourself in the financial aspects of your business, the outcome of going that route will be very beneficial to your business both in the short and long run. You need to make sure you are on the same page as your accountant and also be able to interpret the financial statements. These statements have a lot of managerial guidance that can help you in your decision-making process when used effectively. So, try to be ahead of the game to enjoy the effectiveness of this powerful business operation tool.

Do not forget to market your business to keep current customers with you all the time. Moreover, the techniques help to persuade new customers to join your effort and maximize ROI. All the time, keep evaluating the importance of the ads before you send them to the customers. The significance should be evaluated with consideration of many factors including:

- Coverage message.
- Timing and the length of the ads.
- The media to be used.
- The cost of disseminating the ads.
- The projected outcomes.

When you notice a misalignment of the ads, correct the mistake as fast as you can to avoid burning money and time.

Utilize other techniques for growing a successful business such as working on your strengths and weakness, educating yourself in managerial fields, and others. In the end, you do not just want to be a chief operating office by name, you need to hold that position after knowing all the essential responsibilities that go together with the title and how to fulfill them.

**Congratulation**

**On reading the book to the end.**

**I hope you will start your business soon.**

**I wish you all the best in your new endeavor.**

# God Bless You!

# Last Word Before you Close this Book

Thank you for reading this book to the end.

No matter how hard it is, I believe you can do it. You can become one of the successful businesses in your hometown. It all starts from inside you. The fact is, it is so easy to prove some people wrong when they throw arrows left and right at you. Proclaiming that you cannot do anything tangible in this world.

However, if it is you who is blocking yourself by saying or believing that you are not capable or worth enough to do anything!!!

## That is a barrier you cannot overcome!

Avoid considering yourself as just

## *AN ORDINARY PERSON.*

You are capable of accomplishing anything.

# BELIEVE ME!

## You are better than that.

### TAKE A BOLD ACTION NOW!

### I MEAN, SOONER THAN LATER!

**I wish you all the best in your new journey of becoming a**

# SUCCESSFUL BUSINESS OWNER

We Cannot Become What We
Want By Remaining What We Are!

# Appendix A

## 44 Things to Do Before You Start Your Restaurant Business

| # | Name | Y/N | Comments |
|---|------|-----|----------|
| 1 | Build a business plan | | |
| 2 | Get family behind you | | |
| 3 | Allocate source of fund | | |
| 4 | Get business assistance and training (if needed) | | |
| 5 | Decide on business structure | | |

| 6 | I have already secured a state business license. | | |
|---|---|---|---|
| 7 | I have already acquired a local/city license. | | |
| 8 | I have received an employer identification number (EIN) from the Internal Revenue Service (IRS). | | |
| 9 | My business needs a loan as an additional starting and working capital. | | |
| 10 | I know which financial institution to get the loan from. | | |
| 11 | I have initiated preliminary contacts to secure the loan. | | |
| 12 | I have a business name handy. | | |
| 13 | I have already registered the business name. | | |
| 14 | I have checked the availability of a domain name. | | |
| 15 | I have a website set for my business. | | |

| 16 | For corporation company: I have prepared incorporations papers. | | |
|----|---|---|---|
| 17 | I have called utilities, cable, and phone companies for installation. | | |
| 18 | I have business accounts opened. | | |
| 19 | If necessary: I have applied for a business credit card. | | |
| 20 | I did exhaustive homework regarding payroll requirements. | | |
| 21 | I know where to get help regarding hiring procedures. | | |
| 22 | I am good at accounting requirements for my business including where to get professional help when necessary. | | |
| 23 | I know the number of employees to employ. | | |
| 24 | I have selected my target customers. | | |
| 25 | I have already set the | | |

| | | | |
|---|---|---|---|
| | following areas based on my business model:<br><br>• Dining room<br>• Kitchen<br>• Bathroom<br>• Counter<br>• Storage room<br>• Exterior | | |
| 26 | I have allocated and decided on the target market. | | |
| 27 | Get the right insurance policies, such as:<br><br>• Worker's compensation<br>• Professional liability insurance<br>• Product liability insurance<br>• Business vehicle insurance<br>• Small business health insurance<br>• General liability insurance<br>• Property insurance | | |
| 28 | Get the right tools (if needed) | | |
| 29 | Set up your social media channels (if needed) | | |
| 30 | Order business cards | | |

| | | | |
|---|---|---|---|
| 31 | Understand your duties as an employer | | |
| 32 | Divide key duties:<br><br>• With your partnership(s)<br>• Employees | | |
| 33 | I have already allocated the vendor I need. | | |
| 34 | Look for a mentor (if needed) | | |
| 35 | I know all required codes and regulations of my business, when necessary. | | |
| 36 | I can adhere to all the codes and regulations of my business. | | |
| 37 | I have already set the menus and prices for my business | | |
| 38 | All-important materials have already been bought, install, and functioning accordingly.<br><br>• Cash register<br>• Storage equipment<br>• Cooking equipment<br>• Food preparing equipment | | |

| 39 | The soda fountain has already been installed and it is functioning well. | | |
|----|--------------------------------------------------------------------------|---|---|
| 40 | Arrangements with the trash and grease companies have already been done. | | |
| 41 | Signage has already been installed and is working | | |
| 42 | All marketing strategies and campaigns have already been put in place. | | |
| 43 | I know how the transportation issue will be handled. | | |

# About the Author

The author of this book possesses sold and longtime experience in the business field. He wants to share various techniques and ideas deemed necessary for the newcomers in the business arena. Moreover, for those who have been in this business for a while, there is plenty of knowledge to brush up on your talents to meet the current competitive markets. It would help if you had wide-ranging ideas and techniques to withstand the competition forces that never stop coming from each direction and with different magnitudes.

The author has both academic and practical experiences that he wants to share with you in real-time in your life. Before you start your trucking business, the knowledge conveyed to you will be an eye-opener to understand essential techniques of running a successful business ahead of your competitors.

## Academic Accomplishments

The author has a degree in Doctor of Philosophy in Business Administration (Ph.D.) with a specialization in International Business. The degree empowers the author to perform several research in various areas in the business field. That is why he is more than willing to share some of the results with you while preparing to open a new door to your life for becoming a successful business owner.

## Practical Experience

The author has been spending a lot of time in his life putting into practice the education he got to access its functionality in the real world. He owns many businesses such as; a trucking business, a financial company dealing with tax preparation, without forgetting; a business consulting firm.

# References

Restaurant Industry Outlook For 2022: Five Trends To Watch
https://www.forbes.com/sites/forbesbusinesscouncil/2021/11/10/restaurant-industry-outlook-for-2022-five-trends-to-watch/?sh=5bcc23c6249b

U.S. Restaurant Industry: Current State, Trends & Outlook
https://www.gorspa.org/commiq-us-restaurant-industry-current-state-trends-outlook/

When can the restaurant industry expect to
recover? https://restaurant.org/research-and-media/research/research-reports/state-of-the-industry/

Minimum Wages for Tipped Employees.
https://www.dol.gov/agencies/whd/state/minimum-wage/tipped

Definition of *supply* (Entry 1 of 3). https://www.merriam-webster.com/dictionary/supply

The top 20 food distributors in the USA
https://onlinemasters.ohio.edu/blog/financial-statement-analysis-helps-business-grow/

How Financial Statement Analysis Helps Business Grow Benefits of a
break-even analysis. https://www.sba.gov/breakevenpointcalculator

These Are the Top 10 Fine-Dining Restaurants in America, according to
TripAdvisor https://www.fsrmagazine.com/bar-management/fsr-50-top-10-upscale-dining-chains

Oxford University Press, (1999). The oxford American Dictionary and
Language Guide. Oxford University Press pg. 583

Made in the USA
Middletown, DE
30 May 2022

66414268R00159